GAMES STUDENTS PLAY

GAMES
STUDENTS PLAY

(and what to do about them)

Ken Ernst

CELESTIAL ARTS
Millbrae, California

To My Sons —
Dan, Dennis, Tom, and Mike.

CONTENTS

The Rules for All Games 9
Who Plays 10
SECTION I

Trouble-Maker Games
1 / Disruptor Variety 13
    1. Uproar 13
    2. Chip On The Shoulder 29
    3. Stupid 30
    4. Clown 34
    5. Schlemiel 35
    6. Make Me 36
2 / Delinquent Variety 41
    7. Let's Find 41
    8. Cops and Robbers 43
    9. Want Out. 46
3 / Prelude to Deeper Understanding 49

SECTION II

Put-Down Games
4 / Discount Variety 59
    10. Sweetheart 59
    11. Blemish 60
5 / Complainer Variety 63
    12. Why Does It Always Happen To Me. 63
    13. Indigence 64
    14. Why Don't You — Yes But 66
    15. Late Paper 67
    16. Wooden Leg 69

SECTION III

Tempter Games
6 / Kissy Variety 73
    17. Disciple 73
    18. Lil Ol Me 74
7 / Trap-Baiter Variety 76
    19. Let's You and Him Fight 76

20. Miss Muffet 77
21. Let 'Em Have It . . . . ; . . 79
22. High and Proud 81
23. Do Me Something 82
24. Stocking 83
25. Rapo 84

SECTION IV

Teacher Games
Identifying Teacher Games 91
8 / Close-to-Student Variety 93
    26. Buddy 93
    27. Self-Expression 94
    28. Critique 96
    29. You're Uncommonly Perceptive . . 96
9 / Helpful Variety 98
    30. Student Folder 98
    31. I'm Only Trying To Help You . . . 99
    32. Sunny Side Up 102
    33. Education 103
    34. Why Don't You — Yes But . . . 104
    35. Look How Hard I've Tried . . . 105
10 / I-Know-Best Variety 107
    36. Furthermore 107
    37. Tell Me This 107
    38. Professional 108
    39. Why Did You — No But 109
    40. Now I've Got You 110
    41. See What You Made Me Do . . 111
    42. Courtroom 112
    43. Corner 113
    44. It's Been Done Before 115
11 / Conclusion 116

Appendix
    The History and Development of
    Transactional Analysis 117
References/Bibliography 123

ACKNOWLEDGEMENTS

Thanks are due in general to the students of the psychology classes at Kennedy High School in Fremont, California, for their many suggestions and valuable criticisms. I owe personal thanks to my brother, Franklin H. Ernst, Jr., M.D., who years ago interested me in psychology; and to the late Eric Berne, M.D., author of GAMES PEOPLE PLAY, who gave me this project to do and encouraged its progress. I owe a special debt of gratitude to Mel Boyce, of Marin County, California, an original student of Dr. Eric Berne who wrote the concise history of Transactional Analysis in the back of this book. Perhaps no one is better suited to provide this section: he presently functions as a therapist and also writes and teaches in the "games" field.

Ken Ernst
Fremont, California
August, 1972

THE RULES FOR ALL GAMES

THE WORD "GAME" in this book is used in a specific sense. A game has a seemingly plausible and innocent surface statement, or opening move, which is aimed at getting a sympathetic response from a listener. If this response is given, the game goes into more detailed maneuvers, with two or more players engaged.

The players choose specific rules which are interchangeable, and the play is conducted in a way ranging from passive to aggressive — that is, to a soft, medium, or hard degree. These psychological games are not much like childhood games; they are more closely allied to thoughtful activities like chess, contract bridge, or puzzle-solving.

Every game has predictable causes, moves, and payoffs. Of course, no two games of "Uproar," for example, are exactly alike, any more than any two games of chess or football are exactly alike. But the moves are not random. The informed teacher or parent can spot the rules governing the seemingly random moves made by the players.

The essential characteristic of a game is that it has two levels — one obvious and the other ulterior. Humans are insatiably curious about double leveled puzzles, double meanings, and proverbs. These double levels are the source of much humor; the player of a psychological game, however infuriating he may be, can be entertaining, too.

For every game discussed here an example is given straight from the classroom, an analysis of the moves in the game, and an antithesis (or "stopper") to the game.

WHO PLAYS?

Every parent, school board member, principal, counselor, teacher, and student needs a "game detector." When anything goes badly in school, this "game detector" can help him figure out who is trying to do what to whom and how to stop it, if it needs stopping. *Games Students Play* is designed for this purpose.

Everyone, in effect, plays some sort of game; but some players address themselves to the constructive side of life and should be encouraged, while others are playing for ends that can only be called anti-social. The first problem for any player, of course, is to know what game he is playing, and then to follow the rules as carefully as possible. Knowing them, he can avoid games and get on with more creative objectives.

Here for the first time the "games" played in classrooms are described in the light of Transactional Analysis. This book deals only with "games" in schools; it does not go into what the curriculum should include, since course content and schedule structure are not in the province of a psychologist.

I have grouped the games into four broad categories. The first three present games played by students; the fourth contains games played by teachers. A section is devoted to each of the categories. These are: I. Trouble-Maker Games; II. Put-Down Games; III. Tempter Games; and IV. Teacher Games. Varieties within each category, and all individual games, are listed in the Contents.

1

Trouble-Maker Games

When a "game" prevents teaching, what's your move?

CHAPTER 1

TROUBLE-MAKER GAMES: DISRUPTOR VARIETY

Teachers are paid to teach. Disruptions interfere with the job. What does the teacher do with a disruptor?

Here are six types of disruptors, each playing his distinctive psychological "game."

1. Uproar[5]

The teacher, Mr. Johnson, walked into class on the first day of the new school year. He had taken a couple of summer courses at the university towards his master's degree and still had time to go with his wife and four boys on an extended camping trip. He felt rested; he felt prepared; he felt ready for another year of teaching.

The students quieted down expectantly as the bell rang. They looked up, watching carefully for clues as to what "Old Man Johnson" was going to be like. The word from former students was that he was an easy grader, that his voice tended to be a boring monotone, that his lessons were sometimes interesting. Those rumors were only general information. Each student watched the new teacher's every move, eager to figure out what his opening game plan would be.

After the bell rang, Mr. Johnson put aside a stack of paper work, brought out his class list and began to call roll. He had long ago learned to listen carefully to roll responses. He had learned to listen for the opening move in a long series of transactions that are not happenstance, not coincidental, but as subconsciously calculated as a broken field running by Notre Dame's quarterback. Each student had an objective in mind and a favorite strategy to use. Mr. Johnson, from his years of teaching experience, knew this and watched these early transactions carefully.

Every student, he knew, had long ago learned what to expect from his mother and father and other grownups. Each had learned the best way of getting along in the world of mom, dad, and other big people. In some families whining games would get him the best deal. In others it was the mysterious silent play, in others spontaneity and relaxed exchanges were O.K.

Mr. Johnson began calling the roll. Some students answered cheerfully, some sleepily, some timidly. As he went down the list of names, he heard by the tone of voice and saw by the body position and expression how the youngster felt about his parents when he was five and how he felt now about authorities in general. The whiners, the sullen ones, the relaxed O.K. kids all saw Mr. Johnson through their own pairs of psychological glasses. Some saw him as a threatening persecutor, others as a rescuer, still others as a source of information, a bumbler, or a potential love object. With variations, the teacher is usually known as a surrogate or substitute parent.

Continuing down the roll sheet, Mr. Johnson called, "Dean Forester." A pause and then a sullen, low, "Here." A few names later he came across Denny Dixon's name. Denny's response was silence. A slight smile crept across his face. Mr. Johnson repeated his name. "Oh, here," Denny said in slightly mock surprise.

By the time Mr. Johnson was halfway through the roll, he had a rough idea of which students might play which games. The next name was Muriel Mills. The relative silence was shattered by a multi-decibel, taunting whine, "It's supposed to be Mur-i-ELL." "Wow," thought Mr. Johnson to himself, "a full-blown 'Uproar' player."

Transactional Analysis is concerned with analyzing transactions, with figuring out what is going on between two or more persons. Mr. Johnson called "Muriel Mills" and she shot back with a taunting and deafening answer. One part of the teacher's personality called her name. A part of Muriel's personality answered. To analyze this transaction Mr. Johnson has to work with his matter-of-fact request for information and Muriel's challenging answer. By watching someone's behavior, words, intonation, facial expressions, gestures, and mannerism a person can begin to see basically three distinct ego states or personalities. With practice he can see which of these is in control of a person at any one time.

These three distinct personalities will be shown as three circles:

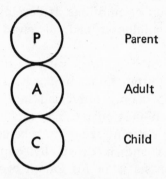

P   Parent

A   Adult

C   Child

The Child ego state or Child personality is the same one the person had when he was a child of eight or younger. It isn't the same as "childish," but childlike – a state that many adults, particularly creative ones, often express. Some people seem to be always coming on as Child; others let the Child part of themselves out only fleetingly.

Already Mr. Johnson is noting how Muriel sits, stands, speaks; he will watch for the Child ego state in her and know what to expect. He found that he did not need to talk at length with each student to get information. They were busy giving him more information than he could use, even when he talked and they listened. He watched Muriel and saw that her head was tipped up and tilted to one side. There were already visible horizontal lines etched on her forehead. Her jaw jutted. Her eyes would snap shut for two or three seconds at a time with the eyeball looking up. She was a perfect example of the defiant Child listener.[12]

So far, so good. Mr. Johnson had spotted her as a defiant Child. He saw a good clue that she was going to play "Uproar." So what now? Each student was watching to see what "Old Man Johnson" was going to be like. With what game would he respond? That's what it means to "psych out" a teacher. What are his games?

The students so far have only seen Mr. Johnson's Adult ego state. The Adult ego state is basically a computer. It receives information through the senses, stores it logically, recalls data, and makes predictions. The Adult, like a computer, has no feelings or emotions. It develops gradually during the years of childhood and, if given a chance, throughout life.

What Muriel and the other students were watching for was Mr. Johnson's Parent ego state. Since by law he is a surrogate parent, each student is mainly interested in the teacher's Parent so each one can manipulate him to his own best advantage. Mr. Johnson's Parent ego state is behavior copied from his own parents and modified by copying other authority figures. When he is in his Parent ego state, Mr. Johnson is like a cassette recorder. He plugs in an old tape that his mother, father, uncle, or someone else gave him. Then he will play it through, often with his father's mannerisms and inflections. This Parent vocabulary includes the words "because," "therefore," "good," "bad," "right," "wrong," "have to," "supposed to," "must," "ought to," "should," and more.

Whenever the words Parent, Adult, and Child are used to refer to ego states they are capitalized. The concepts of Parent and Child can be further divided. The Parent ego state has two basic functions. One is nurturing, taking care of the young and protecting them without qualification. This is a good and necessary function, even though it can be overused to the point of being smothering and over-protective. The other function of the Parent is to act on prejudiced ideas, which have been accepted uncritically, and which came largely from one's own parents, grandparents, and teachers. It is a real advantage to be able to act quickly and without much thought in solving many everday problems; it would be enormously time-consuming to subject every small daily problem to careful rational scrutiny. But the prejudiced or critical Parent can also be overused, filling the person in that ego state with many inappropriate "Do's" and "Don'ts."

Finally, the Child ego state has two parts. The natural or free Child is curious, fun-loving, spontaneous, and creative. The adapted or compliant Child state developed in response to pressure from one's own parents, and acts in ways calculated to please or satisfy them.

Mr. Johnson, or Muriel, or anyone else has only one ego state in control at a time. If Mr. Johnson blew up and raged at Muriel (a distinct possibility), he could at the same time be aware of what he was doing, as if standing beside himself as an observer. While one ego state is in control (in this case the Parent), another ego state has to stand by helplessly and watch.

Muriel, an advanced "Uproar" player, is determined to get all authority figures to play "Uproar" or an allied game. Her opening attack included knuckle-cracking, gum-popping, finger-tapping, pen-clicking, hair-combing, dress-straightening, pencil-sharpening, paper-rattling, clock-watching, coughing, whispering, pencil and book-dropping, paper-tossing, note-passing, turning around, wiggling, coming in late, acting stupid, and trying to sidetrack the lecture.

The Child part of Muriel was "bugging" the teacher with a series of small incidents to force him to blow up at her. If Mr. Johnson controlled his temper, she had him at bay and could continue to goad him until he did blow up. Then she would win; she could complain to her friends, other teachers, the principal, and to her parents that he was "unfair" and had picked on her. Her whole aim was to get a game of "Uproar" going. "After all, all I did was drop my pencil, and he yelled at me."

When will Muriel explode? When do "Uproar" players do their uproaring? All along the spectrum from murderers and rapists to student pests, there is the question of pre-dictability. Murderers don't murder all the time, nor do they murder at random. Students like Muriel don't bug authorities all the time, nor do they bug everyone in authority.

The "who" is easy to answer. The Muriels of the world

will play their games, in this case "Uproar," with those persons who promise the most attention in return. The "when" can be explained by the concept of "trading stamps."

Many people collect trading stamps at their local stores. Some go out of their way to collect trading stamps, some don't collect any. Psychological stamps, like the paper variety, come in regular and giant sizes.

There is a physiological reason for collecting psychological trading stamps. It is that one of the main functions of the brain is to store energy.[3] Sometimes when we can't get what we want immediately we have to wait. We store the desire until we can satisfy it later.

Muriel collected real or imagined insults and hurts. This was her racket, a phony gimmick. She purposely stockpiled them so she could feel justified in throwing an "Uproar" at the teacher, before a guaranteed audience, and gaining maximum attention.

Children learn early how to collect psychological stamps and what to trade them for. A small boy falls down in his back yard and hits his knee. He gets a hurt look on his face. He looks around the yard, runs inside, looks from room to room until he finds Mommy. Now he bursts into tears, cashing in his "feel-sorry-for-self" stamps for a free sympathy. As this boy grows he will become more sophisticated. He will learn how many psychological stamps fill a book and how many books will get one item, such as a depression, a fight, or a fright.

Take an example from class. Mr. Johnson comments that Betsy doesn't look well, and asks if everything is all right. Betsy bursts into a storm of tears. He can't understand what happened unless he realizes that Betsy has learned to collect depression stamps. When she thinks she has enough to fill a book she will trade it in on a mild depression.

The only difference between paper trading stamps and psychological stamps is that the latter can be reused. If a man flirts with a new girl at a party, his girl friend could become angry. Instead of saying something at the time, she can collect anger stamps. She can cash these in over and over again, anything she gets made at him: "And don't think I've forgotten how you act at parties with other girls."

Muriel was collecting anger stamps. Whenever anyone, especially someone in authority, said or did something displeasing to her she took it as a "put-down" or "discount." Muriel collected enough anger stamps to cash in on one free-of-guilt "Uproar." The more books of stamps she collected the bigger the "Uproar" she could trade them for.

What can Mr. Johnson do? Here are some of the possibilities:

1. Blow up and bawl out Muriel, as the Tyrant Teacher might.
2. Suffer in silence, as the Martyr Teacher might.
3. Feel hurt, as the Whining Teacher might.
4. Argue, as the Scrapping Teacher might.
5. Kick her out, as the Impatient Teacher might.
6. Fear her, as the Timid Teacher might.
7. Turn her game off by using the Transactional Analysis suggested in this book.

1. *The Tyrant Teacher.* The Tyrant Teacher blows up and hollers at Muriel in class. He gets her temporarily quiet by overpowering her with words, or in some cases by using force. Though it looks like he wins, she is the real winner of this round. She has proved again that Parent-types are unreasonable and holler a lot. This form of Parent teacher is easy to spot and just as easy to bug.

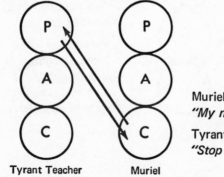

Tyrant Teacher   Muriel

Muriel:
"My name is Mur-i-ELL!"
Tyrant:
"Stop hollering."

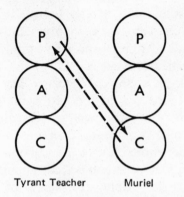

Tyrant:
"Stop hollering."
Muriel:
Temporary silence,
plotting revenge.

Tyrant Teacher   Muriel

Mr. Johnson had better watch out. Muriel is plotting the next moves of her "Uproar" game and is pasting anger stamps in her book. She is sure to cash them in later. In this example, Muriel got Mr. Johnson to respond with Game 36, page 107, "Furthermore."

2. *The Martyr Teacher.* If Mr. Johnson patiently endures the outburst, he can bet money that it will happen again because he has given implicit permission for another outburst. Around his mouth you find the well-etched lines of many hours of teeth-gritting. He is noted for his aspirin-gobbling and for his deep, exasperated sighs. The Martyr, a form of nurturing Parent, is easily spotted, and he is willing to be kicked with snotty remarks of the "Uproar" type.

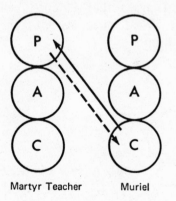

Muriel:
"It's supposed to be Mur-i-ELL!"
Martyr:
Clenched teeth, lips pressed tightly together, deep sigh. Implicit message of suffering.

Martyr Teacher   Muriel

In this case Mr. Johnson is a self-pitier. He collects depression stamps. He seems to carry the burdens of the world. He has a choice of complaining out loud about the bad state of affairs in the world, especially the ingratitude of youth, or he can be more sophisticated and stiff-upper-lip it. An accomplished Martyr can evoke at least one "Isn't he brave?" (or the equivalent) each day. But Muriel is capable of giving out more irritation than Mr. Johnson will ever be able to endure "bravely." He will always lose the game.

3. *The Whiner Teacher.* Mr. Johnson tries to explain to Muriel how it disrupts the class for her to talk out and make noise. He gives her bribes and extra jobs to win her over. This works for a short time, but later she is worse than ever. Now, after all he has done for her, she treats him like this. He feels hurt.

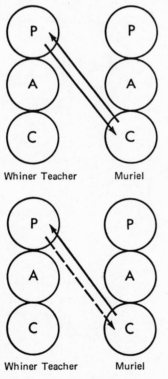

Whiner Teacher   Muriel

Muriel:
Disrupts class.

Whiner:
"Here, why don't you help me take the roll."

Whiner Teacher   Muriel

Muriel: *Calls roll loudly and laughs. Throws the roll book onto his desk from six seats away.*

Whiner: *Hurt expression comes over face.*

If he comes on like a weak Child, Muriel will use him and abuse him at her leisure. While this may work on some persons whose Parent personality is predominant, it won't work on Muriel.

4. *The Scrapper Teacher.* Mr. Johnson, the scrapper, hears a Muriel outburst. While she tries to bug his Parent, he decides to fight fire with fire and replies with a Child retort.

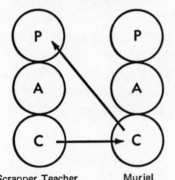

Muriel: *It's supposed to be Mur-i-ELL!"*

Scrapper: *"You sound just like a pet parrot."*

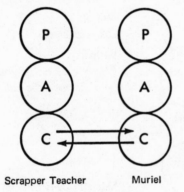

Scrapper: *"You sound just like a pet parrot."*

Muriel: *"Are you an expert on the bird?"*

This can go on for a few exchanges, until the Parent of Mr. Johnson takes over. The main problem with this approach is that a game player like Muriel is expert in her field. Even with practice Mr. Johnson could do no better than a draw, with Muriel still exploiting him.

5. *The Impatient Teacher.* First day, first class, first five minutes. Mr. Johnson hears Muriel being very noisy. "Out!" he says to her.

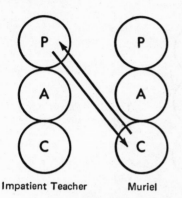

Impatient Teacher   Muriel

Muriel: *Makes noise to bug the teacher.*

Impatient: *"Out!"*

In this case, Mr. Johnson's immediate problem is solved. Muriel's problem is not touched. It is simply moved to the principal's office. While this solution may be tempting to some, it is not the best answer; and if every problem were handled this way the classroom would soon be empty.

6. *Timid Teacher.* Muriel's mouthings visibly shake Mr. Johnson, who is already seen to be an unsure person, a not O.K. type.

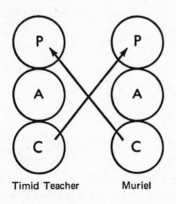

Timid Teacher   Muriel

Muriel: *"It's Mur-i-ELL!"*

Timid: *"Please don't yell. If the principal hears a commotion, he'll think I can't control my class."*

Muriel has two choices now. She can take control of the class by threatening "Uproar," or she can destroy Mr. Johnson by embarrassing him when he is being evaluated or visited.

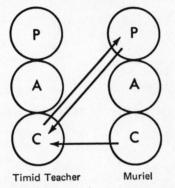

Timid Teacher   Muriel

Timid: *"Please don't yell . . . ."*

Muriel: *(1) Take over the class. (2) Destroy Mr. Johnson.*

Mr. Johnson does not need to consider this method seriously. Anyone who has taught for any length of time knows that a timid Teacher cannot last.

A glance at the diagram shows what Muriel is doing and how she halts the progress of the class. Mr. Johnson is talking Adult-to-Adult. Muriel crosses this transaction with the Child-to-Parent reaction. This crossed transaction is typical of the way misunderstandings occur. All conflicts, from lovers' quarrels to wars, are the result of conscious or unconscious crossed transactions. Conversely, a crossed transaction, if programmed by the Adult, can turn off a game, as you will see Mr. Johnson do with Muriel.

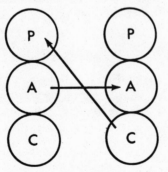

Example of Crossed Transaction

Mr. Johnson: *Is Muriel Mills Here?*

Muriel: *My name is Mur-i-ELL*

Not one of these methods has been "the" winning play or "the" answer to the problem of what to do about Muriel's outburst. This is not surprising. No one way will handle all problems. Some super-strict teachers are excellent with certain students while other students respond well to easy-going methods. Some seemingly disorganized teachers with a dozen projects going all at once in what looks like chaos get great results too. This says that the teaching methods used are not the criteria for good and bad teaching or for "control" or lack of it. "The best and the worst teacher allocate their time among academic pursuits in about the same way."[23]

If none of these "methods" will work, what is going to be the most effective way of turning off Muriel's "Uproar?" Mr. Johnson should now open a copy of *Games People Play,* by Eric Berne, and look up the game of "Uproar." He should look for the reasons people play this game, and very carefully the antithesis, or how to turn off the game. The first order of business is to figure out why Muriel plays "Uproar." What does she get out of it? This is no mystery to any parent or teacher. She wants attention. Mr. Johnson may ask himself, "Why does she need so much?" "Why from me?" "Why in such a negative way?"

To best understand the answers to these questions let us first remind ourselves of what a child needs to be physically healthy. His hungers are for food, water, warmth, and strokes. Structure hunger is explained in Part II. The first of these, food, is obvious to the degree that government agencies pay all or part of the cost of school lunches in some districts. If a child is hungry and his stomach is growling, math is meaningless. Second on the list is water. If a student is parched he can't keep his head on history. Again governmental agencies have seen the necessity of paying for drinking fountains. Third, a reasonable temperature is a requisite for learning. Heaters are installed when it's too cold, and in some areas air-conditioning for excess heat or humidity. This brings us to strokes.

Check out this idea for yourself. Imagine how it would be to go through an entire day saying "Hello" to the people you would normally greet and find that nobody responds to your greeting. How would you feel? An easier way to check (but not necessarily a recommended one) is to completely ignore someone else. How would he react? These verbal strokes to which we are so accustomed have power and importance. The "Hi," "Harya," "Howzit," "Hlo," and many others may not seem like much, but take them away and watch the disaster. The hunger each of us has for even these minimal attentions is comparable to any of our other hungers. When we do not get enough, we become painfully aware of it and go to great lengths to remedy the lack.

Rat experiments show that physical, mental, and emotional development and even the biochemistry of the brain are favorably affected by handling and stroking. What is more striking, these experiments showed that gentle handling and painful electric shocks were nearly equally effective in promoting the health of the animals.[26] The 1945 published work of Rene Spitz[30] showed that small children need actual physical stroking. Just as different people acquire tastes for different foods, they also acquire a preference for different kinds of strokes. One student may work hard for praise strokes for his academic work. Another may not care about academic achievement but lives for the laugh strokes he receives for his zany antics. Muriel has cultivated a taste for being-hollered-at or being-punished strokes. Anyone can figure out that if she stopped "Uproaring," teachers would not lash out at her or punish her. Obviously since she "Uproars" often she must be after the end result. As the examples show, she is an expert at maneuvering teachers into giving her what she wants. The next step for the teacher is to stop the "Uproar" game. Mr. Johnson takes steps to turn off Muriel's "Uproar."

1. He confirms that she is an "Uproar" player, by checking the records and talking to last year's teacher and others

who know her. If she gets punished regularly for noisy and provocative behavior, he can be sure that she is a game player.

2. He tells her in a calm and firm Adult voice to see him after school. This is a critical point. Mr. Johnson has practiced his Parent, Adult, and Child voices, using a tape recorder to learn the difference. Muriel is looking for a Parent voice, so he must take special care to be clearly Adult.

3. This step is taken when Muriel comes in after school. It will only be effective if made without a Parent criticism. Remember that if Mr. Johnson is in his Parent ego state it will show in his voice, his face, and in his posture. Mr. Johnson tells Muriel about the game of "Uproar" and explains how the game interferes with work and interferes with friendship.

4. Mr. Johnson explains that he is a teacher and that he is paid to help students learn. He must also prevent disruptions.

5. He tells her that school is like a free supermarket. The student can go in, load up, and leave without paying because her parents have already paid. If Muriel does not like the grocery clerk she can get even with him by not taking the goodies, or she can ignore her dislike for him and load up anyway.

6. Mr. Johnson does not reply directly to any of Muriel's "Uproar" comments. His reply is to listen. Active or reflective listening gives verbal feedback of the content and a guess at the feeling implicit in the spoken words or acts.[24] Mr. Johnson might say to Muriel's complaints, "Class seemed boring today and you are angry at having your name mispronounced. Is that right?"

7. The final step is for Mr. Johnson to establish some sort of rapport with Muriel or get another faculty member to do so.

This last step is more than a "nice" gesture. It offers Muriel an alternate way of getting her strokes. Mr. Johnson did a bit of inquiring about her interests and discovered that she was quite gifted in art. He made a visit to the art room and saw some of her work; he then mentioned it to her, expressing a genuine appreciation of her works, without overstating or gushing. Within a week the "Uproars" were greatly diminished in his class. By the end of six weeks they had stopped altogether. Mr. Johnson continued to say "hello" on campus and ask about Muriel's art work. Her art work was excellent and there was no need to make faked or forced compliments which are always spotted as such.

No student can be expected to do his best if he is hungry, thirsty, too cold or too hot, or if he hasn't had enough strokes. Lack of strokes is the cause of many lost man hours when we try to force or entice students to learn in junior high schools and high schools. Most of them are in the puberty and early romance stages, when there is a shift in the persons from whom they get their strokes. Trying to buck this hunger and energy is a waste of time. Better to use it whenever possible. Whether in language, math, history, or science, use examples from the students' life content and use their names. This will give good strokes as an alternative to having to play games for strokes.

One of the best ways of spotting what is going on in a game is to figure out when a student or teacher repeatedly does something, what is the predictable result? This result is what he wants. Muriel keeps bugging teachers. People yell at her. That is what the Child part of her wants — the extra supply of strokes, more attention. It is healthy to give her strokes but not yelling, "Uproar" strokes. Muriel is an "Uproar" player with sixteen years of experience. Mr. Johnson has to remember that he is not likely to change her life style. What he aims for is to knock off the disruptive part of the game in his classroom.

In looking at the examples presented above, many have come to the conclusion that a teacher on the job should maintain an Adult ego state at all times. Not so. Imagine an entire class conducted by an uninvolved, emotionless computer. The result: instant boredom. The Adult needs to be monitoring what the Parent and Child do. If a student disruptor player does appear, then flip the master switch to Adult and avoid the time-consuming and wheel-spinning game maneuvers.

2. Chip On The Shoulder

A second student, Dean, played games that superficially resembled Muriel's. Many students were afraid of him. He threw things, made double-entendre remarks, and caused just as much of a ruckus as Muriel. Mr. Johnson asked Dean a question at the end of the first week of school, "Can you say in Spanish, "a girl'?" Instead of trying to answer Dean said, "No, but I can French a girl." He then glanced suggestively at a pretty girl and stuck out his tongue at her. This disrupted the class and drew attention away from Dean's inability to answer the question. Spankings by the principal, talks with the parents, and detentions did not even slow him down. The principal of the school had a policy of asking teachers to get to know and work with "problem" students. Mr. Johnson was asked to work with Dean. He found after several months that the boy had been worried that he would look "dumb" in class in front of his friends if he tried to answer questions. He decided he would rather be known as "Dean, the Devil" than "Dean, the Dumb-Dumb." The teachers did not notice that he was particularly slow because he had an amazing repertoire of sexy and insinuating remarks at his command.

His game may look like Muriel's, but it is not the same. Muriel actively looks for someone to bug. Dean only causes a problem if you knock off his "Chip On The Shoulder," whether accidentally or on purpose. In Dean's case the sensitive spot, the "Chip On The Shoulder," was a low I.Q. To cover up he lashed out.

Antithesis: In contrast to Muriel, who actively looked for openings to bug Mr. Johnson, Dean was not at all interested in bugging the teacher. He was concerned with not looking dumb. Mr. Johnson, the Spanish teacher, and Mr. Yamamoto, the science teacher, cooperated by giving him the job of constructing a Spanish mission. He worked on this for several months and did a good piece of work by any standard. Dean deserved and received sincere Parent and Adult strokes for his work, strokes such as "I'm proud of you" and "That's an excellent job." The teachers were more Adult with him instead of critical Parent. The teachers helped him get through school while suffering nothing worse than irritation at a curriculum which was often irrelevant to him. Ten years later he is a stable citizen with a steady job and a happy marriage.

To generalize from Dean's case, the way to avert this problem is to find out what the student is trying to avoid and then offer him a mutually acceptable alternative. Besides those like Dean who are afraid of looking dumb, there are hyperactive youngsters and creative ones who find themselves stifled. These often also play "Chip On The Shoulder."

3. Stupid[5]

Denny seemed to dislike himself. His smile made you think he has just done something bad and you don't know about it yet. His parents called on the principal to ask that the teachers be gentle with "little Denny." The parents feared that he might have brain damage and had taken him to the University Medical Center for several tests. The test readings were inconclusive. At school he would do "Stupid" things in and out of class. One of his "Stupids" was holding the bat by the fat end in a game of baseball and letting the pitched ball hit him in the face. The others got angry and called him "Stupid." One rescued him, saying "It's not his fault." Once he brought his history book to Spanish class "by mistake." On several occasions he did the wrong page of homework. He made clumsy and "Stupid" moves in every endeavor he tried. Each time he made one of his "Stupid" moves he watched to see if he was going to be laughed at or called names. It was not long before many of the students were actually calling him "Stupid" as a nickname.

Mr. Johnson soon noticed something incongruous about Denny's behavior. Every time he did a "Stupid" and was ridiculed, he smiled slyly. After some observation the pattern emerged.

1. Denny would look for an audience.
2. He would make a dumb move.
3. Others would make fun of him.
4. Denny would smile.

Some of these transactions were rapid, taking no more than a few seconds. Others were elaborate productions taking several weeks. For example, Denny went to great lengths to check books out of the library for a term project. He did some reading and took some notes. Each step of the way he showed Mr. Johnson what he had accomplished. Halfway through he began to taper off, but he was careful to let the teacher know of his dwindling interest. When the time came to turn in the work he washed his pants at home. In the pants pocket was the pack of three-by-five cards containing all his notes.

Mr. Johnson could be trapped by Denny here. If he is hard on Denny and refuses to accept his excuse he will be thought of as a mean Persecutor. If he laughs at Denny, he will also be a Persecutor. On the other hand, if he tries to be a good guy and gives Denny special treatment, Denny will see him as a Rescuer, a patsy he can take advantage of. In several other games Mr. Johnson has noticed this same pattern. Denny and certain other game players have categorized people into two groups: the Persecutors, who are mean, cruel, and punishing, and the Rescuers, who are patsies, pigeons, pushovers, people who "try" to help. No matter what his father, teacher, friends, or others say, Denny always manages to put each of them into one category or the other. Games played from the Persecutor or Rescuer position reinforce the idea that other people — children, Catholics, blacks, virtually any group — are not O.K. people. Games played from the Victim position reinforce the idea that the player himself is not O.K.[24, 25]

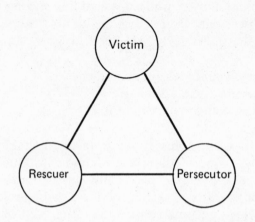

Antithesis: One day on the playground Mr. Johnson asked Denny, "When did you first start conning your parents into thinking that you're "Stupid?" Without his customary sly look, and without his usual lisp, Denny said, "About two years ago." No attempt was made to cure him of the game, and his grades did not go up. However, he no longer played his game in Mr. Johnson's classroom.

Denny's object was not to bug the teacher as Muriel did, or to cover up a real or imagined failing as Dean did, but rather to call attention to himself and especially to have people kick at him verbally. He could manipulate those around him into reinforcing his position; in this case, an "I'm not O.K. − You're not O.K." position. His "Stupid" actions push others into being irritated or over-protective. A friendly confrontation is an effective antithesis.

How did Muriel and Denny get started doing what they do? They know the consequences of their actions, so why have they chosen this way of getting strokes?

Mothers and fathers do their best when bringing up their children, but unconsciously and despite their best efforts some parents unwittingly do pass on unfortunate games to their young. The mechanism for this is the control of strokes. Since mother and father control the supply of attention or strokes in the child's early years, they can demand a high price for them. Youngsters, as they grow up, are stroke-hungry. They spend most of their waking hours working to get strokes from those who have the supply, namely their mothers and fathers and later their teachers.

If a youngster has learned to get strokes for "messing up," "being bad," or "being "Stupid" there is sometimes a giveaway or clue that you can spot with practice – the gallows transaction. This is an inappropriate smile on mom's face when her son does something wrong. When Denny did something "Stupid" at home his mother smiled wryly as she scolded him, "How many times do I have to tell you to watch your step?" Denny is working for the smiles he gets. An inordinate amount of anger will work as well. Either of these strokes, the inappropriate smile or anger, is a super stroke because it comes from THE important persons to a small child, his parents.

If you know a "Stupid" player, watch and see if some people do not smile when he does one of his "Stupids." These smiles give him encouragement to do it again. The "Uproar" players and all the rest of the game players are going through the moves in their games for one reason – it is the method they have learned for getting their strokes.

The reasons why and when strokes are given or withheld from children are of vital concern. There are a number of taboos concerning strokes. If a boy gives another boy or a girl gives another girl a warm stroke, eyebrows are lifted, giggles exchanged, and comments made. There are taboos that prevent stroking between men and women outside a pre-scribed relationship, such as going steady, or being engaged or married. There are taboos against physical touching between grownups and children unless they are in the nuclear family, and then only under certain circumstances.[34] The whole process of "raising children" is one of giving and withholding strokes to ensure that the children maintain the parents' values.

Self-styled crusaders have attempted to get certain books out of school libraries, certain courses like sex education out of the curriculum, and certain teachers off the faculty. The more fanatical the crusaders, the more he shows himself to be committed to unhealthy games.

4. Clown[5]

Sam, the "Clown," was well-liked by teachers and students in and out of class.

One day shortly before Mr. Johnson was to arrive for class, Joe turned around and said to Sam, "Hey, do your imitation of Mr. Johnson."

"O.K.," said Sam, "lend me your glasses." He walked out of the door with books, notebook, keys, and glasses. He opened the door casually, slouched in, dragged himself up to the front of the room, flopped his books and keys down. Then he took the notebook and rummaged through it. He fumbled in his pockets for a pencil. He put the glasses down on his nose and peered over them. "Who has a pencil?" he droned. He borrowed one. He called on one of the students, who were by this time roaring with laughter at this clever caricature of their teacher.

When the lookout whispered, "Teacher's coming!" Sam grabbed his books, keys, and notebook, and made a frantic dash for his seat. All was quiet when Mr. Johnson opened the door casually, slouched in, and reenacted the previous scene all to the silent amusement of the class.

Sam will rarely be a problem in his class. He is only interested in having people laugh at him and in proving that he is harmless.

Antithesis: In the strictest sense Sam is not playing a game. He is being a "Clown" to get attention or strokes, but he is doing so in an open, honest way. Mr. Johnson resisted the temptation to be angry and "Uproar" at what looked like insolence. Instead he expressed appreciation of Sam's artistry.

5. Schlemiel[5]

Betty walked into class late. Mr. Johnson asked her for a pass. She stopped next to Karl's seat and searched in her purse for it. Just then Karl's face lit up as he found an interesting item in the book he wanted to discuss. He raised his arm and hit Betty's purse. "Oh, I'm so sorry," he pleaded. He got down and began picking up the items from Betty's purse. In the process he bumped Winnie's desk so that her papers became scattered. Again he apologized profusely, and in trying to pick up Winnie's papers he stepped on her report and ripped it. Winnie blew up at him for being so clumsy. Karl put on a silly grin and went back to his seat muttering, "She doesn't have to be so snotty. It was only an accident."

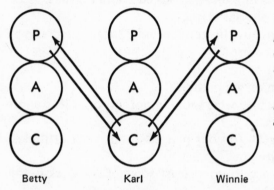

Betty   Karl   Winnie

Karl: *Knocks Betty's purse to the ground and rips Winnie's report.*

Betty *"That's all right, don't worry about it."*

Winnie: *"Well, watch it."*

Either way, Karl wins. One way he gets a "that's all right" permission from Betty to "Schlemiel" again. The other way he can feel treated unfairly by Winnie and can complain that "It was only an accident."

This is another example of a game where the game player has categorized others as either Persecutors or Rescuers. Each time Karl does a "Schlemiel" he will "mess up" something of someone else's. He will watch each response to each action to see how to categorize it. When Betty forgives him for spilling her purse he interprets the forgiveness as permission to do it again. When Winnie gets angry over her report being ripped up, he interprets this as a Persecutor remark that he will exploit as "unfair."

Antithesis: It is difficult to manage a friendly confrontation with a "Schlemiel," because a "Schlemiel" will be likely to find a Persecutor remark in any confrontation. But it is not likely in most classes that there is much equipment or material that can be messed up. In a science center or foreign language center, Karl should be told plainly and in an emotionless Adult voice not to handle or touch any equipment. To the charges of "unfair," Mr. Johnson should answer, "true," or "I agree." To date, this has satisfied classroom "Schlemiels."

6. Make Me[5]

Mr. Johnson said as the class started, "Please pass in your assignments." Collecting them, he asked Laura for hers.

"I didn't do it," she answered.

"You'll have to turn in your weekly assignments if you expect to pass the course."

"I don't care."

"Don't you plan on graduating?"

"Maybe if the course were more important or at least more interestingly presented."

"I'll have to speak to your parents about your attitude."

"Go ahead. I dare you."

"Look, you'll have to do at least some of the work in this course."

"Why don't you try and make me?"

"You'd like that, wouldn't you?" says the girl behind her.

Here is still another example where the game player busily puts others into the rules of Rescuer or Persecutor. If Mr. Johnson backs down, Laura wins. She has proved again that men can be made to look foolish and can be backed down easily. If Mr. Johnson accepts the challenge and "makes" her do the assignment, she will prove that he is a mean, tyrannical Persecutor. If he is seen as a Persecutor, she can further indulge in some of her early fantasies about men forcing her to do things against her will.

This game can also be seen at dances, in hallways, and other places where boys and girls meet and talk. In the mild form, the girl says, "No," but her tone of voice, tilt of head, and facial expression tell him that this "No" means "Yes."

In the hard form, the girl openly challenges the boy and his masculinity. "Betcha you can't make me," or "You're some kind of sissy." Or she can openly laugh at his masculinity. She can force some boys to back down. If one stands up to her, he sets himself up for a game of "Rapo." This girl knows only the two types of men, Rescuers and Persecutors.[25]

With a teacher she may challenge his masculinity, but she is more likely to challenge his authority.

Antithesis: To a "Make Me" player, the antithesis to the game is for the teacher to set up clear choices and consequences. If Laura does the work, fine. If she doesn't do the work, that's her problem. At the beginning of a course Mr. Johnson posts the amount of work needed for a certain grade. He also sees that each student is appraised of his progress at frequent and regular intervals. Laura will try to hook Mr. Johnson's concerned Parent ego state into making such statements as, "What *I* want you to do is this." If the teacher inadvertently makes such statements, then the work is seen by the student as being the teacher's work and doing it is for the teacher's sake.

Another way of eliminating this game is doing away with letter or number grades. One such possibility is that the student proceeds in courses such as foreign language and math at his own rate until he has accomplished a set goal. Instead of being given a C, D, or F he is given more time to reach a higher standard of proficiency.[20] In artistic and creative areas such as writing and painting, the student can keep the finished project as a demonstration of his work for the year, semester, or course. If the project is bulky or perishable, pictures or even microfilm could be used instead of a transcript.[15] Since the student himself is the one who decides whether or not he will succeed, he might as well have a part in deciding what to study and how far and how fast to go.

Summary of the Disruptor Games. All six students playing Disruptor games behaved in similar ways. Each one, for example, called attention to himself with the class as an audience. But what will turn off one game will not turn off another. The key as to what to do about these behaviors is to find the payoff of each game. As a student goes through the moves of his game, watch to see what the payoff is each time. Is the payoff an "Uproar?" Is the payoff appearing rebellious? Is the payoff getting applause and laughter from an audience? Is the payoff being bawled out or getting permission to continue being clumsy? Is the payoff having the teacher force the student to do something?

Looking back over these disruptor students we can see that although they may all act alike in some ways. They do so for reasons that are quite different. Muriel is, psychologically speaking, wearing a sweatshirt that says, "Don't Argue With Me!" Dean's shirt says, "Leave Me Alone!" Denny's says, "Don't Call Me 'Stupid'!" Laura's says, "Don't 'Make Me'!" Sam's says, "Laugh at Me!" Karl's says, "Don't Be Angry!"

Muriel's, Denny's, Karl's, and Laura's sweatshirts are the most provocative by far. The provocation is the big challenge "Don't." The Child ego state in each of us has a built in rebelliousness that is easily triggered to action by a repeated "Don't." From the time Pandora was told, "Don't open the box," and Eve was warned "Don't eat the apple," we have found it difficult to resist the forbidden.

Stressing the forbidden in a "Reverse Message" can be a powerful invitation to do it.

"The last thing in the world I want is . . . ."

"Don't ever let me catch you . . . ."

"How many times do I have to tell you to . . . ."

Reverse these messages and you have what the speaker is covertly saying. This is an invidious method of getting people to do things. Overstress what not to do. Then when they do the forbidden they will end up with a load of guilt, and guilt is a powerful mechanism for controlling people.

Widespread use of the "Reverse Message" can, and does, sensitize youngsters to resent being forced or made to do anything. This causes the compulsory attendance laws, for example, to be resented by the very ones it was supposed to protect. In some respects the teacher is put in the same resented role as a guard in a prison. Consider the number of "Don'ts" now common in schools.

"Don't smoke."	"Don't take drugs."
"Don't fight."	"Don't get out of your seat."
"Don't cut class."	"Don't speak out of turn."
"Don't chew gum."	"Don't hold hands."
"Don't fall."	"Don't whisper."

To many students this heavy emphasis on the "Don't" becomes a challenge. Only a small challenge is needed to set some students off, whereas others will not respond until an inexperienced substitute teacher takes over the class.

The school says, "Don't smoke." Teachers are given patrol assignments to enforce the edict. Those students whose parents taught them by the "Don't-Don't" or "Reverse Message" method are quickly tempted to smoke. Here they find the familiar Persecutor strokes of authority they learned to look for as small children. There are also the strokes of encouragement they can get from friends who play the same game.

Occasionally a psychology student figures out how he is being used in these games by those around him, his family and friends. It is startling to see a sudden reversal of behavior in such a student. But a game player who hasn't read *Games People Play* is not in command of the situation even though he imagines he is. He is no more in command than a bull charging a cape in the arena of a bullfight. He has been set up for the kill. This is most obvious in the complementary games of "Now I've Got You" (NIGY) and "Cops and Robbers."

Another example is the girl saying, "I really do love my boy friend" while she is shaking her head meaning, "Not really."

"I'll try," often means the opposite of "I'll do it." One student told Mr. Johnson how much he liked the subject he was taking, and at the same time slammed his fist into his palm. The whole technique of the "Reverse Message" is typified by the fairytale character Abe, who always said the opposite of what he meant.[2]

Each game player works his two to five major games over and over and over. The experienced teacher will know the effective antitheses that turn off these games. He further develops a repertoire of rejoinders for stopping the disruptive games and the potentially dangerous games. An inexperienced teacher usually relies more on Parent-type answers. These tend to be nonadaptive cliches from the prejudiced Parent. These cliches are what the teacher's own father or mother said when exasperated. These statements are occasionally effective, but they are more apt to continue a game because of the built-in Parent-to-Child nature of the response.

Anyone who is new to the concept of games should constantly remind himself that each game player is working for strokes and is an expert with training and years of experience. In the case of the student, he knows how to trigger the teacher's prejudiced Parent to anger or impatience. But practice and patience will prevail if these two rules are kept in mind:

1. Resist the temptation to give the payoff the game player is working for. Don't "Uproar" with an "Uproar" player. Don't hit the sensitive chip off the "Chip On The Shoulder" player. Don't call a "Stupid" player "Stupid." Don't blame or forgive a "Schlemiel." Don't force a "Make Me."

2. Give some kind of appropriate strokes to these players before the next game gets started. Let each player know that you think he is O.K. There is no person who does not have some strengths, some qualities worth a genuine compliment. If this is done sincerely over a period of time without being overdone, it will short-circuit the destructive portions of games.

CHAPTER 2

TROUBLER-MAKER GAMES: DELINQUENT VARIETY

7. Let's Find[5]

Steve didn't go out of his way to cause trouble, but he *looked* like a "hard guy." He rode a motorcycle and wore a cutoff Levi jacket. He had several other motorcycling friends, one of whom was Eddie. Neither cared much for homework, class discussion, or tests. One morning Steve sauntered down the corridor past room 52. He dropped a paper and stooped to pick it up. As he did so he glanced casually around. Seeing no one in the corridor, he pulled out a knife and jimmied open the door. Picking up the phone in the room he dialed room 58. In his best imitation of a "front office" voice he said, "This is the front office, could you please send Eddie O'Rourke down here right away? It's important." A minute later, Eddie was slipping into room 52. He and Steve were saying, "Let's Find" something to do. After several suggestions Steve remembered he had a cherry bomb in his locker, and they were off to get it, throw it in the principal's office, pull a fire alarm, and light a fire in a trash barrel.

Although it is a close relative of "Cops and Robbers," "Let's Find" is not so much part of a script, or life-plan, than it is a juvenile attempt at structuring time. "Boys will be boys" is the cliché expressing our expectation that boys of a certain age will get into a certain amount of mischief. Dennis the Menace is an example at the elementary school level. Racing cars up and down the main street is a high school example. Goldfish swallowing, phone booth cramming, and certain political activities are examples at the college level. All are examples of the rebellious Child functioning at these ages.

The "Let's Find" game described here is common because structuring time is a particular problem to those under legal age. Some will go to the movies, others will build models, others will work or play an instrument. If his script has him cast as a "bad guy," the "Let's Find" player will find something to do of a juvenile delinquent type. This is especially troublesome when it leads into games such as "Uproar" or "Cops and Robbers."

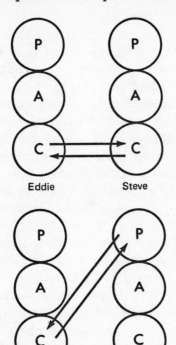

Eddie

Steve

Eddie & Steve   Principal

Eddie: *"Whatcha wanna do?"*

Steve: *"I dunno. What do you wanna do?"*

Steve: *"Hey! I've got a cherry bomb in my locker. Let's toss it in the Principal's office."*

Eddie: *"Great! Let's go!"*

(They toss a lighted firecracker into office and run.)

Principal: *Becomes angry (prejudiced Parent) and calls in all the "known trouble-makers" and questions them.*

Steve: *"I didn't do anything! It's not fair for you to accuse me!"*

A "Let's Find" player often spends more time vandalizing and stealing then he does on many constructive jobs. His position is "I'm not O.K. and you're not O.K." He collects stamps that he can cash in on dirty, sneaky tricks.

Antithesis: Mr. Johnson formed a school-sanctioned motorcycle club. Those who might have gotten into more trouble were now busy working on their bikes and planning trips and parades. The only effort at therapy was to show by example the benefits of "getting on with life,"[14] of making headway toward desired and realistic goals in life. A four-year follow-up showed that not one of the boys who was active in the club got into trouble with the police. The motorcycles were an alternative way of structuring time. Each individual or group would need to find its own alternative. For some blacks the Black Panthers have provided special ways of structuring time that reinforce a more O.K. position.[31]

8. Cops and Robbers[5]

Frank and a couple of his friends were in the sophomore locker area. Two teachers approached. Frank, with a cherubic expression, said, "Psst, here come some teachers." This was loud enough for the teachers to hear. There was a sound of lockers slamming and from behind the lockers emerged a crowd of students in a cloud of smoke. Most of the students crowded around the two teachers.

"Why're you two coming by here? We aren't smoking," said Frank.

"We're scheduled to patrol this area now," said Mr. Johnson.

"You can't prove anything unless you catch us with the cigarettes." Mr. Johnson made no reply to this. "What would you do if you thought I had cigarettes on me?"

Mr. Johnson replied, "If I saw you with cigarettes I'd have to turn you into the office."

"Well, I don't have any in my shirt pocket," said Frank with a sly grin on his face.

Mr. Johnson didn't comment.

"These aren't cigarettes," Frank said as he pulled the shirt lightly over the pack in his pocket. These words had a trace of exhilaration woven through them. Mr. Johnson put his hand to his head to scratch his chin. At that move, Frank jumped back, ready to run. He saw the teacher make no move to grab at the outline of the pack of cigarettes. He stuck around for a while quietly watching the group talk. After three minutes of pastimes and some Adult information exchange he stepped forward and pulled a cigarette out of his pocket. Mr. Johnson said he was going to turn him in. Frank took off running and laughing. The others asked, "Why don't you let him slide this time?"

Mr. Johnson said, "I may not agree with the law, but if I don't turn him in I'm breaking the law." Frank was later suspended and complained, "It ain't fair."

Mr. Johnson was required by the system and forced by Frank to play the cop role of "Now I've Got You." Mr. Johnson's view of the transaction was that it was a crossed transaction.

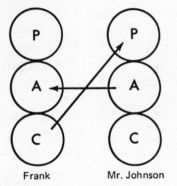

Frank: *"What would you do if I told you that I had cigarettes in this pocket?"*

Mr. Johnson: *"If I see anyone who is not of legal age with cigarettes at school, I have to turn him in."*

Frank's view of it was:

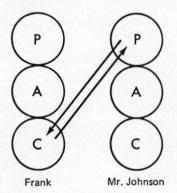

Frank: *Pulls out a cigarette in front of Mr. Johnson.*

Mr. Johnson: *Turns him in. This is seen by Frank as a punishing Parent action.*

Frank has a "Not O.K." position. He sees authorities as Parent types. They are either suckers and Rescuers or punishing Persecutors. In the above case, if Mr. Johnson had let Frank get away with breaking the rule, then Frank would have seen him as a sucker. When Mr. Johnson turned him in, Frank saw him as mean and unfair.

Antithesis: These "getting nowhere"[14] people are difficult to work with. For short-range immediate results, repeated Adult transactions are the most effective. Mr. Johnson told Frank, "If I see someone illegally smoking, by law, I have to turn him in. If I don't, I am breaking the law and could get into trouble myself." Along with immediate Adult instructive transactions, Mr. Johnson used a long-range Parent effort to encourage Frank, and made interested Adult comments and inquiries about Frank's healthier interests.

The Parent comments might include, "I was really proud of you Frank when you got that A." The Adult comments might include, "I was impressed by the work you did on your car, Frank."

Delinquent games are especially likely to be played by those who are having identity problems. To help in establishing his identity to himself and others, every growing youngster makes some identifying mark on a wall, a piece of furniture, or a tree. As he grows and proceeds through school he will decide on a series of best ways to "leave his mark."[13] Some options are to paint a picture, to write an essay, to get on the honor role. These can be done with glowing pride. Other options are to vandalize a classroom, to get in trouble, to carve on a desk. (Proudly displayed at Disneyland in Anaheim, California, is Walt Disney's old grade school desk with a couple of W.D.'s boldly carved in it.)

If a delinquent game player leaves a mark he is assured that his mark is more likely to be permanent. If Frank gets caught, for example, a permanent record will tell of his adventures with cigarettes. These records are even locked up and guarded, so they can be seen as having extraordinary value.

One high school posts each morning a list of all the "bad" students who have "earned" demerits. Some students look on this as their honor role.

Other schools have provided an area such as a fence, a wall, or a portion of pavement explicitly for marking. These schools report that vandalism has been reduced. The effectiveness of this technique depends on how prominent a position the area enjoys. The pavement in front of one school that contains the markings is much more effective than the fence hidden toward the back of another school.

This is not always an easy antithesis to vandalism to put into effect. Walls, for example, have at least six functions:[13] environmental shielding; soundproofing from outside (keep the playground noise from distracting); soundproofing from inside (what would the principal think if he heard the noise?); sight proofing (privacy); prevention of intrusions; confining of persons inside. Some school personnel feel strongly that walls should also be esthetic, or "in good taste" — which will always provoke disagreements.

One thirteen-year-old boy gave up setting fires when he was given permission to draw on the wall. Burned marks were not as satisfying as wall drawings for leaving his mark. Also, making his mark in secret was not as appealing as marking it in public.[13]

Many educators have asked, "Why don't some students want to make good marks (grades)?" Could it be that they lose interest because the markings taught and encouraged are not permanent? By the time many students get to school they have been trained to not make marks. The teacher further trains them to use non-lasting chalkboards and paper. These get cleaned off or thrown away. What is the point of sweating over a term paper if it is unlikely to be permanent?[13] Permanent records of achievement and projects are vastly preferable to codified grades.[15]

9. Want Out[5]

Mr. Johnson handed Hoppy a worksheet. Hoppy said he wasn't going to do it, and repeated this challengingly. Mr. Johnson sent him to the office, and Hoppy was kicked out of school. He seemed jubilant and told his friends that he was going to "have a ball." He said he hated school and couldn't wait to get out. The next day, however, he was at school staring in the windows at his classes. Finally he sneaked into a couple of his large lectures.

One educator has estimated that the percentage of students "kicked out" of school who return for all or part of the period of suspension is roughly 3 per cent. This 3 per cent comprises the ones who play "Want Out." All their actions indicate that they "Want Out" of school, but when suspension gets close, they talk the dean into "one more chance" or they sneak back onto the campus.

Mr. Johnson let detention hall out at 4:20 p.m. If the room was quiet, he let the students out as much as 20 minutes early, depending on how quiet it was. The 3 per cent playing "Want Out" said that they "Wanted Out" early, but they made noise at the very moment they were about to get out. This was usually enough to ensure keeping the class at least a few minutes late.

Any student who truly wants to leave school has several options for getting out. He might use:

Permanent explusion
Varying lengths of suspension
Pregnancy
Marriage
Dropping Out
Sickness
Running away from home
Cutting
Graduation
Getting an outside job as part of the curriculum

If any student claims to "Want Out" of school, and uses one of these or other methods and comes back, then he's probably playing "Want Out." Even if he comes back against his will, he might well have maneuvered himself into the situation.

Antithesis: Mr. Johnson spotted Hoppy as a "Want Out" in his class. Before each subsequent class, he took care to say "Hello," and to ask some "caring" questions of him. Before Hoppy could start some maneuver to get himself kicked out by the teacher's prejudiced Parent, Mr. Johnson turned on either the nurturing Parent or the fun-loving Child or the interested Adult.

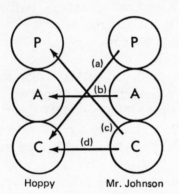

Hoppy   Mr. Johnson

a. Nurturing Parent to Child; *"Hi, Hoppy, how are you doing? Are your studies coming along all right?"*

b. Adult to Adult: *Any interesting news will do.*

c. Child to Parent: *"Hoppy, I have a problem with my car. Do you know much about carburetors?"*

d. Child to Child: *A joke can work well.*

CHAPTER 3

PRELUDE TO DEEPER UNDERSTANDING

Disruptors usually aren't subtle; their goal is to gain the attention of an audience, and they'll use anything, from acrobatics to a bullhorn, in order to achieve it. In the quieter areas of game playing, however, stand millions of pupils who offer only the faintest evidence that they are wearing masks. How can these more subtle players be understood? How, for example, can Mr. Johnson tell the difference between the student who understands and the one who is only pretending to understand? How can he tell if he is really teaching?

Mr. Johnson knows from all his courses in education that there are approved methods for finding out. Some of these are: midterm and final exams; surprise quizzes; term projects; class participation; asking questions; heuristic teaching.

Testing, however, often sets up a challenge to cheat, or at best to memorize. Quizzes take up valuable class time. After the Socratic questioning technique, or heuristic teaching, the next best method for knowing at the time whether students are listening and learning is to observe physical clues.

In a classroom setting, the biggest immediate problem is knowing whether the students are really listening, hearing, or whether they are pretending or confused. Some clues to this question are physical. It is instinct to turn up the corners of the mouth when happy, and turn down the corners when discontented. We wrinkle the forehead, lift eyebrows, and so on in accordance to the feeling or emotion being fed into the brain. Cultural conditioning is superimposed on these instincts.[16] The following are nine ego-state clues that pertain at least to the United States.

1. The listener with his Adult ego state in charge will tend to have his head vertical to the ground, his mouth line horizontal often with the mouth closed and teeth touching, head slightly turned for better triangulation, his gaze shifting from location to location, and his eyes

blinking every three to five seconds. His body position
lasts up to five minutes. [12, 28]

2. The impatient Child is restless, and easily spotted in
large lectures. He turns toward the speaker, then away,
then back to the speaker again with gross body, trunk,
and limb movements. He doesn't focus attention in any
one place for long. This compliant and defiant behavior
is often in response to training in the rules of politeness,
expecially the injunctions "don't point" and "don't
interrupt."[12]

3. The pouting Child is secretly listening more intensely
than he lets on. He is defiantly compliant. His face is
tilted slightly forward. His gaze and face is averted. He is
secretly peeking at the person the pout is for.[12]

4. The coy Child has his head down and turned at a slight
angle away from the speaker. He looks up for brief
glances from the corner of his eyes.[12]

5. The embarrassed Child has coloring in his face. This is
accompanied by decreased attentiveness or jerkiness of
movement.[12]

6. The defiant Child has his head back during his defiance
He may have horizontal lines on the forehead. The face
muscles are often flat or emotionless. He is a non-
listener.[12]

7. The interested Child's eyes are open wide and the pupils
are dilated.[16]

8. The prejudiced Parent ego state often has a scowl with
vertical forehead lines. His head is tilted. Sometimes he
has a horizontal head shaking movement.[12]

9. The nurturing Parent has his neck forward somewhat.
His head is tipped forward and tilted to the side a bit.
His eyebrows are raised. This is often accompanied by a
head nodding or approval motion. If he does this while
talking, he is saying to you, "What I am telling you is
important for you to know. It is for your own good. I
mean for you to learn this." If he nods while listening,

he is telling you, "I completely agree with you." He is also telling you that he thinks that you need encouragement.[12]

These are only clues, of course. The meaning of a posture is contained in its relation to the context.[8] Even though a word in a sentence has meaning, only in the context of the sentence is its complete meaning seen. The same is true of looks, glances, stares, and other uses of the eyes.[27]

Many of these physical clues are so slight or quick that they are almost subliminal. But the subconscious of some persons can detect these signals of body language with amazing accuracy. This is one element of intuition and should be fostered.

Every teacher has noticed at times a nodding "Kissy" in the front row. This "Kissy" is either working for points or feeling sorry for the incompetent speaker.

Even though some students are busy writing letters, sending notes to friends, or gazing out the window, they may also be understanding the material of the lesson. This is possible if they have their Adult turned on to the lesson.

One girl, Tessie, was known by everyone at school as pushy and insolent. One day the teacher was giving the lesson. Tessie was just sitting down after having walked around for a while. Another front-row girl said, "Oh, that Tessie! She hasn't paid any attention and she'll never learn anything." Mr. Johnson, who knew the physical clues to whether a person is listening, told the girl, "Tessie heard everything that we talked about today, and she understood it too." Tessie watched the teacher in wide-eyed amazement. Slowly a grin spread over her face and she told in precise terms what had been discussed during the class. Conversely, the student who has his Parent or Child turned on may be playing games that interfere with learning.

The student, and the Child part of him, does not arbitrarily or capriciously set out to annoy the teacher. He is trying to control his environment. This is one of the first tasks for any infant. The most important parts of his surroundings in the early years are his parents. Baby learns how to make mom and dad happy, angry, disappointed, sad, resentful, and more. Baby grows up and goes to school. He sees the teacher as another parent. The law says the student has to be there and the teacher is responsible by law. The teacher tells him what he should and should not do, just as his parents can. By the time the student reaches the classroom he has had years of experience in learning to control his parents. It would be surprising if he did not use these environment controlling techniques on his new environment of school.

Some remarks by teachers that can easily trigger games are:

"What *I* want you to do for *me*. . . ."

"*I* was disappointed in. . . ."

"*My* assignment for tomorrow is. . . ."

More effective and less gamey is to put the emphasis on the student's efforts:

"*Your* idea is impressive."

"What would happen to *your* idea if *you*. . . ."

To avoid a certain class of games Mr. Johnson tells his students the same thing he told Muriel, "School is like a store. You're given a cart and can load up with as much as you want. Your parents are paying the bill. If you decide you want to hurt your parents, and you do it by not loading up your own cart and not taking anything for yourself, then that is your problem, and I'm not going to worry. I've been hired as a clerk in the store to serve you because I've had specialized training in this department. If you don't like one of the clerks in any department you have your choice. You can load up anyway, or you can 'show him' by not taking anything for yourself. It's up to you alone to decide what information and how much information to take off the shelves for yourself."

Anytime there is a disruption in the classroom, it is caused by a crossed transaction, which can easily be diagrammed in the manner of the one on page 24. If the student can hook the teacher's Parent, then the listening, learning, and teaching will stop. To be an effective educator, the teacher must be in a flexible position, able to use whatever ego state is needed.

Each student sees and hears those things that fit his script and the games in it. No psychological game is played alike twice, anymore than two chess games are exactly alike, but the patterns, the rules, and the positions remain the same. Similarly, every teacher and student "figures out" each other within the first few meetings. Each has his favorite games and pastimes with which he is comfortable and in which he is relatively successful.

Each game a student plays will be played only as long as the teacher and/or the students also play. Learning about the games that are played in the classroom will help to turn off the ones which interfere with education.

When there is a problem in class there are several things which can be done. The teacher might: "reason" with the student; kick him out; have the principal or dean discipline him; call his parents; send in a referral to the school psychologist; send him to a counselor.

There will be cases in which the teacher cannot turn off the turmoil. The choice of action cannot be random. Each action must be antithetical to the specific game. What games a person plays is determined by the person's script, or unconscious life plan, and his position, or how he sees himself or others.

As a baby grows, he learns what the world is like, and he will tend to see the world as those around him see it. He will also look upon himself as do those around him. If his parents want him and love him and see him as a success he will think of himself as O.K. If the world around him is one of love and trust, he will see the world as O.K. The type of games a student plays depend upon the position he has decided to take. These four positions are:

I'm O.K.   — You're O.K

I'm O.K.   — You're not O.K.

I'm not O.K.   — You're O.K.

I'm not O.K.   — You're not O.K.

The "You" mentioned can stand for all people, poor people, black people, young people, or any other group. For each of these positions there is an equivalent solution for problems.[14]

For those in the "I'm O.K.–You're O.K." position, the solution is predominantly "Get-On-With"–that is, with people, projects, and life.[14] These are the relatively game-free people.

For those in the "I'm O.K.–You're not O.K." position, the solution tends to be "Get-Rid-Of"–that is, get rid of people and projects.[14] These persons tend to be paranoids.

For those in the "I'm not O.K.–You're O.K." position, the solution to problems is "Get-Away-From."[14] These persons tend to be depressed types.

For those in the "I'm not O.K.–You're not O.K." position, the solution is apt to be "Get-Nowhere-With."[14] These persons tend to be schizophrenics.

Each problem or job has four types of solutions. The difference between the problem student and the learning student is a matter of the percentage of "Get-On-With" or winner solutions he uses.[14]

A person's position is arrived at through early traumatic experiences, which set the stage for the Child to make decisions about life and people. He may, for example, have been frequently beaten and then abandoned by his father and handled ineptly by his mother, giving him cause to believe that "people are not O.K." If he is later mistreated by a surrogate, his beliefs are confirmed and hardened into a position, which he then sets out to demonstrate or prove throughout his life. Maslow refers to such acts as self-fulfilling prophesies.

This position has a more far-reaching effect when, as a teen-ager, the person settles on his script, which is composed of what-to-do-in-life kinds of decisions. Hence, a mildly paranoid person may actually decide to work with people in a helping profession such as social work, to demonstrate his belief that "people cause you trouble," this being his personal slogan. A hard "Ain't It Awful" player may choose the path of juvenile delinquency and early death.

Since games are played by most people and appear in all areas of human experience, it is important to identify them and deal effectively with the dangerous parts of them. It is possible and feasible to confront the game player with his game activity and help enable him to control his behavior—in transactional analysis terms, to help him knock off the game. Given social control and some insight into the situation, the game player, whether a student or a teacher, can develop an antithesis to the game. The antithesis amounts to a restatement of position. The antithesis to the game of "Ain't It Awful" becomes "The great majority of people, including minority groups, are law-abiding and decent citizens," or more simply "People are O.K. most of the time." In the case of "Wooden Leg," where the player's thesis is "What do you expect of someone with a 'Wooden Leg'?" the antithesis is "What do you expect of yourself?"

People play games for a variety of reasons, the most important of which is to avoid intimacy and confirm a lack of trust in others. Other reasons are to avoid responsibility, to be "one-up," to cover up fears and phobias, and to structure time. Berne explains that the structuring of time is one of the greatest tasks that humans face, and that there are only six ways to do it:

1. withdrawal
2. ritual
3. pastimes
4. games
5. work
6. intimacy

These can be defined as mutually exclusive. They are largely self-explanatory, but Berne includes physical, emotional, and psychological behavior under withdrawal, such as daydreaming in class. Rituals refer to formalized procedures. These include the usual weddings and graduations and may also include some private rituals, such as habitual patterns upon arising in the morning. Pastimes merge into games, but are exemplified by conversation which maintains contact but also keeps the other person at a fixed social distance, for example, men discussing cars and women trading recipes are not being intimate because they reveal or involve very little of themselves. Games include other people and at a deeper level. Work may or may not include others but only on an Adult level. Intimacy is a total commitment of self to and with another person on a here-and-now basis.

Shakespeare is famous for his views on human behavior. His line, "All the world is a stage. . ." is commonly quoted and has a ring of truth to persons who know about games. It refers to scripts, which are, says Berne, "a more complex operation—based on an extensive life plan—after the theatrical scripts which are intuitive derivations of these psychological dramas."[4]

Romeo and Juliet played a hard game of "Poor Me," based on an "I'm not O.K.—You're not O.K." position. Their scripts were based on a lifetime of war and social conflict, and their gravestones might well have borne the epitaph offered by Capulet: ". . .poor sacrifices of our enmity."

II

Put-Down Games

How to respond to psychological one-upmanship.

CHAPTER 4

PUT-DOWN GAMES: DISCOUNT VARIETY

10. Sweetheart[5]

Take an insult or a hurt for someone, disguise or sugarcoat it, and you have the game of "Sweetheart." The reason for sugarcoating is the rule of politeness. Many parents tell their offspring not to be disagreeable. "Nice girls don't do that, do they?" The little girl being asked this question has three options:

1. Silence. That, however, is rude. She is supposed to answer when she is spoken to.

2. Disagreement. That, however, is impudent.

3. Agreement. She is constrained to agree by the rules of politeness.

Here we see the adapted Child ego state being trained into acquiescence.

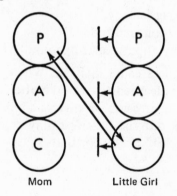

Mom: *"That's right, isn't it, Dear?"*

Little Girl: *"Yes, Mommy."* *(All other comments are blocked.)*

The only way to disagree and at the same time be compliant is to disguise the disagreement. At school, this can take the form of joking. Connie said to Stacy, "You're ugly, (slight pause), I'm only kidding." Stacy was unsure whether to get angry. After all, Connie was only kidding. If Stacy were to get angry, she would expose herself as a touchy sorehead.

Very mild versions of "Sweetheart" are used as friendly banter among friends. When open intimacy is prescribed among men, the recourse is sometimes feigned hostility, expressed in roughhousing or insults. The way to tell if it is friendly or if it is "Sweetheart" is to check with your own Child ego state. The Child is usually perceptive about the psychological level meaning of a comment. The Child listens to the inflections and watches the subtle facial muscles to catch the meaning. If the comment sounded like a hurt to you it probably was. On the other hand, if a large number of people sound like they are trying to hurt you, then it is time to check for paranoia and see whether you are playing "Kick Me." Other "Sweetheart" remarks are: "I hate to say this to you, but . . . ."

"I wouldn't tell you this except that I'm your friend."

"I admire your effort to grow a mustache."

"Isn't it nice that they are putting some style in the larger sizes now?"

"What you seem to be saying is . . . ."

"You poor dear, you don't look well today."

"I don't care what others say about you, I like you."

Antithesis: This is a harmless game in itself. When it is pulled on Mr. Johnson, he has learned to not take offense at the remarks. He refuses the depression or anger stamps. He looks at the comment, picks out the "nice" candy coating part and thanks the "Sweetheart" player for that.

11. Blemish[5]

Certain so-called perfectionists are looking for the "perfect" man or woman, a Prince Charming or Princess Rosebud. Before a perfectionist becomes close to anyone he looks for flaws in the person, whether physical or psychological. This "Blemish" player is not O.K.; he does not feel at ease unless he is around others who are at least as not O.K. as he is.

"Blemish" is a frequent companion of the game of "Rapo," in which one finds a fault or a "Blemish" and uses it as an excuse to tell someone, "Get lost, creep."

Depressive types are especially likely to collect depression stamps from this put-down technique, which is a common method of distancing used by someone who is afraid of intimacy. Closer relations are first encouraged, but when the person comes closer the Parent panic-button is pushed and the "Blemish" is used as ammunition.

Helen, an aloof girl, used social status, education, color of skin, comeliness, and acne to keep a distance between her and any potential friend. "He's not the greatest on looks," or "He has yucky pimples." Literally anything can be used as a "Blemish."

Certain principals and department heads are also known to play this game. Mr. Prince I. Pal drops in for an observation of Mr. Johnson. During the class Mr. Pal busily takes notes and after class hands a copy of the evaluation to Mr. Johnson. On it are the comments, "Window unopened," "Bulletin boards unchanged from two days before," "Teacher coughed during class," "Magazines piles on table in back of room." Checking all the teacher evaluations written by Mr. Pal, one finds that the preponderance of them have this fault finding in them. Mr. Pal does not feel that he has evaluated unless he has found a "Blemish."

Antithesis: The more timid and less O.K. Mr. Johnson is, the more likely that Mr. Pal will keep the "Blemish" tacked on him. Mr. Johnson, however, used his Adult to check out his boss before he started work at the school. He learned his job description well and kept his activities within it. Finally, he kept the authority diagram of the school district in mind to avoid being made the victim in "Now I've Got You" or "Blemish."

On the class level, as with Helen, "Blemish" generally presents no disruption for the teacher; it only disrupts Helen's social life.

Summary of the Discount Games. "Blemish" and "Sweetheart" are games in which an abundance of negative strokes are handed out. These strokes are also called Discounts or Cold Pricklies.[33] Mr. Johnson's classes did some research over a period of three years and found that on the average if a Warm Fuzzy[33] or good stroke is handed out, the chance of getting one back is only 50 per cent. If a Discount or negative stroke is handed out, however, the chance of getting one of these back is nearly 100 per cent. This fact, plus the many taboos on giving warm strokes, go far to explain why games such as "Sweetheart" and "Blemish" are so prevalent.

CHAPTER 5

PUT-DOWN GAMES: COMPLAINER VARIETY

12. Why Does It Always Happen To Me (WAHM)[5]

Mr. Johnson was lecturing. He wondered why four of his students who seemed so capable did so little. During class discussion time he gave Colleen a list of her make-up work, and with big eyes she said, "Why pick on me?" Within minutes a slip came from the dean's office saying she had detention time to serve and a slip arrived from the library reminding her of an overdue book. "Why does the dean pick on me? There were three others who were with me and he didn't do anything to them. But me? I can't even breathe without getting detention. I've never even checked this book out 'Why Does It Always Happen To Me?' " she whined.

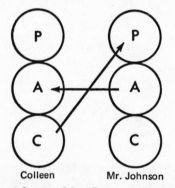

Colleen: *Fails to turn in homework.*

Teacher: *Gives list of work to be done.*

Colleen: *"Why does it always happen to me?"*

Antithesis: Mr. Johnson gives choices of types of assignments and amounts of work to be done. Each student picks out or devises his own program and signs a contract for the amount of work he wants and the grade he wants. Mr. Johnson has student assistants who keep each student aware on a weekly basis of his progress in filling the contract. A highly skilled WAHM player will always find a way to play and thus feel that others are picking on him. This antithesis keeps WAHM to a minimum, and removes the teacher from responsibility for anyone's trying to play it.

13. Indigence[5]

Mr. Johnson called Chuck in for a conference.

"You're not doing well in class. You're not doing the work for me. I can see on your records that you're quite capable of getting A's without straining yourself. You're a senior now, and you'll need these credits to graduate. Would you like me to help you?"

"Yeah, that'll be swell."

"Well, I've gotten a reading list, and if you check out and read three of these books and do reports on them, you can pass the course with a C. Will you do that?"

"Sure."

"All right, let me know about your progress."

Three weeks later Chuck hadn't checked in. Mr. Johnson called him back in and asked, "How are you doing on your three book reports?"

"Not so good."

"Have you read the books?"

"No. I went to the library but they were all checked out except for the first one."

"Have you read that one?"

"Well, it's kinda hard."

"If I can get a week's extension on this, can you try and finish at least one report?"

"Sure."

If Chuck had actually done the work and Mr. Johnson felt good about having helped, there would be no game.

If Chuck had done little or no work, but Mr. Johnson had felt O.K. because he had done his job in helping, then there would still be no game. This assumes that Mr. Johnson had assessed the difficulty of the books and checked out Chuck's ability to handle them. But if Chuck didn't perform and Mr. Johnson felt frustrated, there was a game.

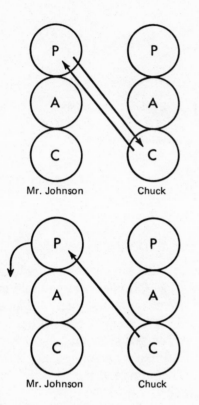

Mr. Johnson: *Tries to help ("Look How Hard I'm Trying.") or ("I'm Only Trying to Help You.")*

Chuck: *Fails.*

Chuck: *Fails.*

Mr. Johnson: *Feels Frustrated.*

Chuck's payoff is proving that Parent-types fail. Certain student "Indigence" players keep up a minimal amount of effort. They keep "trying" and perhaps even "making progress," because in this way they can keep the Parent-types trying to help almost indefinitely.

Antithesis: Mr. Johnson had defined the job of the teacher and student well at the beginning of the year. He had a contract set up with each student. He and each student negotiated the contract as to how much work would be involved, what type of work, and the pay (grade). Both signed the agreement. This affords a better chance for the student's Parent, Adult, and Child to be involved.

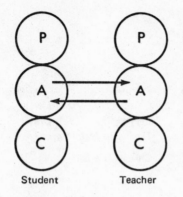

Student: *I'm willing to put out X amount of wouk and I want a certain grade.*

Teacher: *Agrees.*

14. Why Don't You — Yes But (WD-YB)[5]

Lenny was talking after class with two teachers and six students. Lenny brought up a subject, homework, and said he could never get his own done on time. Mr. Johnson volunteered, "Why don't you do it as soon as you get home? Get it out of the way and enjoy yourself after that."

"Yes," interupts Lenny, "but I'm always hungry and want to grab a bite to eat first. Then there's my favorite TV program."

"Why don't you study after dinner?" offered Mr. Johnson.

"I have to do my chores then."

"Why don't you go off to a room by yourself to study?" a friend suggested.

"I have to share my room, and there are no quiet rooms at my house."

"You could go to the library, couldn't you?"

"I'm not allowed out after dinner."

Silence.

"Why Don't You — Yes But" complements the game of "I'm Only Trying to Help You." It reinforces a Parent-to-Child relationship between the teacher and the student. Lenny always felt that everybody tried to dominate him. This was one technique of proving to himself that others, especially Parent-types, could not tell him what to do.

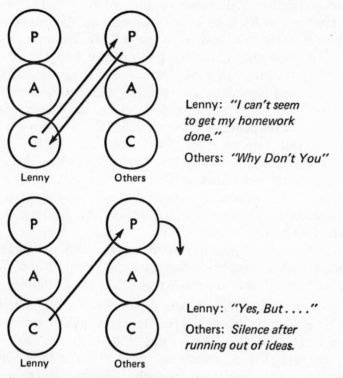

Lenny: *"I can't seem to get my homework done."*

Others: *"Why Don't You"*

Lenny: *"Yes, But...."*

Others: *Silence after running out of ideas.*

Antithesis: Lenny uses his own failure to "bug" his parents. When he fails, they feel awful about it. In Lenny's case his game of WD–YB can be turned off by refusing to give him suggestions as soon as it becomes clear how he uses them. One way to turn the game off is to say, "That seems to be quite a problem, Lenny. What do you plan to do about it?" This way the problem is turned back where it belongs for solution. WD–YB is just as often played by teachers, principals, counselors, school boards, and parents.

15. Late Paper[5]

The class handed in term papers to Mr. Johnson. As Bob left he went by Mr. Johnson's desk and said, "I'm sorry; I didn't turn my report in today. I'll have it in soon." Then he hurried out the door.

Bob was absent the rest of the week. The following Monday he was back in school but without the paper. He said, "I'm sorry. I'll have it in soon." Mr. Johnson, after being put off several times like this, felt as if Bob was toying with him. Mr. Johnson took Bob aside and said that if the paper was not turned in within the week, it would not be accepted. The date came and went. A day longer was allowed. Still no paper. Mr. Johnson said at that point not to bother about turning it in. This time Bob had his older brother phone Mr. Johnson. The brother told him that the father had suffered a heart attack and the whole family had been upset. The brother explained that Bob had taken over a major share of running the family affairs. Mr. Johnson then removed all his time limits.

In spite of the legitimacy of the heart attack excuse, Mr. Johnson had a nagging feeling of being manipulated. The game of "Late Paper" is a relative of "High and Proud."

Antithesis: Mr. Johnson sets a due date for assignments. This date is set deliberately a few days earlier than necessary. When "Late Paper" players come with their excuses, Mr. Johnson says that he always has time to listen to see if it might be a new one not previously published in the great Excuse Encyclopedia. This is not done with heavy sarcasm, but with an appreciation for an artist and his work. "Is it all right to turn in my report a few days late?" is given the matter-of-fact reply, "Do your best."

In addition, Mr. Johnson has assistants whose job it is to remind each student what he has done, what is left to do, and when all his deadlines are.

Another antithesis is to have more flexible scheduling in the school. There are schools in the Los Angeles and Napa areas in California which allow each student to progress according to his ability. If one student can master ten concepts in mathematics within three months, he is allowed to go on to the next course immediately without waiting for the other students. If another student has mastered only five concepts by the end of the year, he is shown his progress and given more time to master the other five. How much more time is dictated by how long it takes the student. Instead of one student getting an A and another getting an F, both can master the subject and get good grades. Time is removed as a factor in grading. Students in these schools have done extraordinarily well in comparison with those in schools with a more traditional grading system.[20]

Still another way of reducing the game playing in schools is to abolish letter grades. Each student could be helped to create the best work of which he is capable in each field. In English class, perhaps a composition could be worked on. The forming of paragraphs, spelling, library skills, capitalization, and the rest would be an integral part of writing some project, a project which at the end of the course would be kept as a permanent part of each student's record. Microfilm is not that expensive, and the added incentive to a student to leave his work in the school with his name on it would be worth the added effort. This would do away with a second-hand and admittedly subjective grading system.[15]

16. Wooden Leg[5]

Mr. Johnson walked into his classroom and looked over the shining faces. In the front row was Maria, a serious-faced blind student. Toward the back was Josie, a pretty, dark-eyed girl in a wheelchair. She had been in a car accident when she was small, and her legs had never healed properly. A third girl, Cindy, was quiet and sat very primly in a corner. She had a pretty face but didn't talk to anyone, volunteer in class, go to dances or football games.

Mr. Johnson had told the class that extra credit could be earned by giving oral reports in front of the class. Maria and Josie were among these who decided to do the extra report. Today was the day, and they took their turn with the others. They were nervous, but no more so than any of the others who got up in front of the class.

After class Mr. Johnson asked Cindy why she didn't do a report. Her grade could have used a boost and the assignment was on geography, one of her favorite subjects.

"I can't," she said quietly.

"Why?" asked Mr. Johnson.

"I've never been able to talk in public."

"Why is that?"

Exasperation at such a question was written on her face, and a tear was in the corner of her eye. Cindy said, "Oh, you wouldn't understand." She turned and walked off.

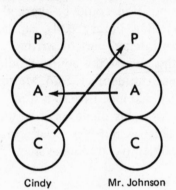

Cindy   Mr. Johnson

Mr. Johnson: *"You can do an oral report."*

Cindy: *"How can you expect someone with a stammer to talk in public?"*

A blind girl and a girl confined to a wheelchair were able to get up in front of a class. But a girl with a stammer couldn't, and this led Cindy to use her disability as a convenient excuse.

Antithesis: Mr. Johnson took the easy way out here and gave Cindy an alternative assignment; this didn't "cure" her of playing the game, but like many antitheses it defused the game as it affects learning in the classroom.

Whenever Mr. Johnson talked to Cindy privately, he said in an Adult voice, "Talk clearly!" On hearing this she would slow down, would speak more deliberately, and would lose her stammer. The stammer was only in her adapted Child ego state.

III

Tempter Games

How to answer subtle players.

CHAPTER 6

TEMPTER GAMES: KISSY VARIETY

17. Disciple

The two versions of "Gee You're Wonderful Professor" (GYWP) are easy to spot but not always so easy to tell apart. One version is "Disciple." Mr. Johnson was finishing his lecture. In the front of the class Ruth sat enraptured. He handed back to her a long extra-credit report she had done on the League of Nations. He said how impressed he was with the report and asked her some questions about certain parts of it. She answered knowledgeably. Again he told her how impressed he was, and she beamed. Two weeks later, Mr. Johnson passed his counselor's examination and was transferred to another school. A middle-aged woman, Miss Spencer, took over his class. As soon as he left, Ruth's efforts and her grades dropped from a straight-A average to barely passing. She daydreamed and lost interest.

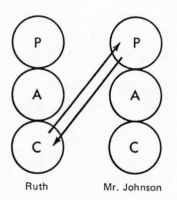

Ruth   Mr. Johnson

Ruth: *"Look what a good job I did for you, Daddy."*

Mr. Johnson: *"That's a good little girl."*

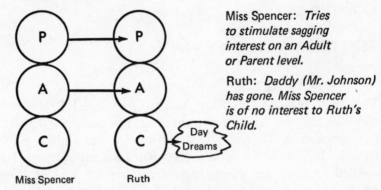

Miss Spencer: *Tries to stimulate sagging interest on an Adult or Parent level.*

Ruth: *Daddy (Mr. Johnson) has gone. Miss Spencer is of no interest to Ruth's Child.*

Antithesis: Miss Spencer called Ruth by name and spoke to her when she saw her on campus. With some patient effort she intrigued Ruth's Child with interesting material. Ruth's grades were up to B's within six weeks.

18. Lil Ol Me

The other version of GYWP is "Lil Ol Me." Vicki sat in front of the class and played "Kissy," nodding in agreement with everything her teacher, Mr. Johnson, said. After class, Vicki went up to the teacher and said how much she had enjoyed the lecture. She asked him to explain a technical term he'd used. He gave a brief definition and examples. She said, "Oh, now I understand. You know, Mr. Johnson, since I've taken your history class I've decided to major in history in college."

"That's fine, Vicki."

"How did you like my comments in class today?"

"They were good comments, worth an extra five points for your daily participation."

As Vicki turned to leave, a knowing look came on her face that told anyone who could see her that she just put one over on the teacher. This classroom version of "Lil Ol Me" is often called "Kissy."

Antithesis: A nodder or a Kissy is often saying, "Shut up" or "I can manipulate you."

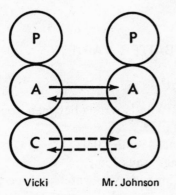

Social Level:

Vicki: *"You're so right."*

Mr. Johnson: *"You're Uncommonly Perceptive"*

Psychological Level:

Vicki: *"I can manipulate you."*

Mr. Johnson: *"I know what's going on but I'll take it for what I can get."*

As long as Mr. Johnson recognizes this as a game he can refuse to be manipulated.

CHAPTER 7

TEMPTER GAMES: TRAP-BAITER VARIETY

19. Let's You and Him Fight[5]

Kim asks her friend Betty, " What's wrong between you and Linda?"

"What do you mean by that?" replies Betty.

"I'd better not say anything." says Kim.

This is not the end, for Kim retires to watch and see what happens between the other two.

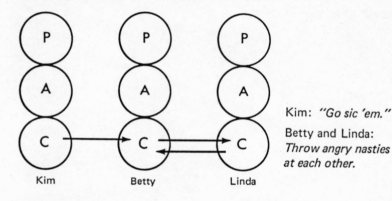

Kim: *"Go sic 'em."*

Betty and Linda: *Throw angry nasties at each other.*

Kim collects throw-up stamps. Often she can be seen to verbally throw-up in class. "I have an item I'd like to throw out here for comment." Watch for a phrase such as "I've heard that some scientists say that all boys who get in trouble and break the law are tied to mommy's apron strings." Like Kim, the trap-baiter usually then backs off and watches the offended persons clean up the mess, in this case the verbal mess.

Antithesis: The way to turn off this game is to toss the "throw-up" or "mess" question back to the source. If Kim says, "What do you feel about the argument that abortions are legalized murder?" you might answer, "What's your

76

opinion?" In the milder form, where Kim says, "I'd better not tell you what she said," the best thing to do is to agree, "You're right. It's not a good idea to repeat some things."

20. Miss Muffet

"Miss Muffet" is a passive relative of "Now I've Got You" and "Let's you and Him Fight."

Mr. Johnson finished his lecture to a high school senior class on current world problems. The class was discussing the causes and effects of the assassination of President John F. Kennedy and Martin Luther King, Jr. Mr. Johnson said that if anyone was interested in more information there was an article in a recent copy of *Playboy* magazine. Linda had been daydreaming and mentally drifting between dress shops, school dances, and the class discussion; when she heard the word *"Playboy,"* she snapped to attention. She always waited for some indiscretion to drop her way. When it did, she either became huffy with Parent-type indignation or actually got her parents involved.

In this case, Linda went home and told her mother excitedly that the teacher was trying to get the class to look at *Playboy*. The parents responded. Her father stormed into the classroom the next day, exclaiming that sweet little youngsters (patting Linda on the head) shouldn't be subjected to such filth. "Why I've read the latest issue from cover to cover twice and it's all filth, just trash." "I'm forming a parents' committee tomorrow night at the PTA meeting to have you fired," said the mother. Mr. Johnson apologetically tried to explain but couldn't get past the barrage of words from the angry parents. Then, with Mr. Johnson still sputtering, the parents stormed out with Linda in hand. In an extreme case of this kind, a mother attacked and stabbed the teacher.

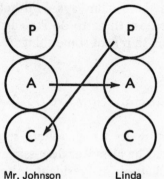

Teacher: *"If you'd like more information there's an article in* Playboy."

Linda: *Tells parents and they come back with accusing and pointing index finger.*

Teacher: *Tries to defend his his actions.*

Mr. Johnson   Linda

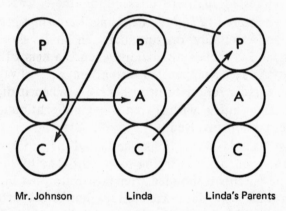

Mr. Johnson   Linda   Linda's Parents

Antithesis: As a precaution, the teacher should know his job description and limits, and he should know the authority structure of his school and district. Anytime he approaches a limit on his activities, he should check with the appropriate superior. Some instructors who wish to talk on controversial subjects or use controversial material have panels of experts review the subject and decide upon its suitability beforehand.

When Linda's mother and father become punishing Parent-types, Mr. Johnson shouldn't defend himself like a guilty Child. Instead, he should let them "Parent" a while until they start to sputter. Then he should offer an Adult assessment.

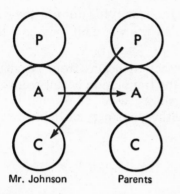

Mr. Johnson   Parents

Parent: Playboy *is dirty.*

Mr. Johnson: *You feel that the article on the assassination of King and Kennedy is pornographic?*

Most probably the parents will try to reestablish a Parent-Child transaction. If they can manage to get Mr. Johnson's Child to defend the article, the magazine, or his own actions, they will continue. If they are unsuccessful in hooking Mr. Johnson's Child, they will quit.

21. Let 'em Have It

"Let 'Em Have It" is a cross between "Miss Muffet," "Kick Me," and "Let's You and Him Fight."

Bernie Philips came up to Mr. Johnson before class. He looked over his shoulder and said, "How are things, Mr. Johnson? Warm enough for you?" Mr. Johnson looked up and mumbled, "Huh? Oh, sure, Bernie," and went back to his work.

With a half smile on his face, Bernie moved closer and began small-talking, getting little or no response. After several weeks of this in class and in the hall the teacher became irritated and told Bernie to make an appointment if he wanted to see him, because it was irritating to be interrupted all the time when he was busy. Bernie went home that night and told his father and mother Mr. Johnson said he didn't like him.

The next afternoon Mr. and Mrs. Philips came to school to complain to the teacher about how he was picking on Bernie. Mr. Philips had a knowing smile playing around his mouth all the time he was talking to Mr. Johnson. "It's not fair the way you treat our boy." The father's voice was a bit loud, and the mother's had a whine in it.

In "Miss Muffett" the transaction begins from an angry Parent. In "Let 'Em Have It," the transaction begins from the Child; "It's not fair" is the slogan used. If the teacher is hooked by this, he will play either the angry or the suffering martyr type of Parent.

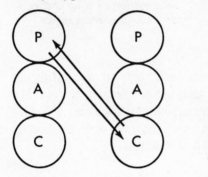

Bernie: *Pesters teacher.*
Mr. Johnson: *"I'm busy. Make an appointment."*

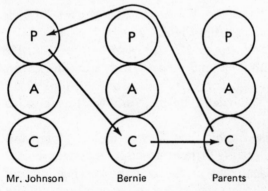

Mr. Johnson: *"I'm busy, make an appointment."*
Parents: *"It's not fair the way you treat Bernie."*

Mr. Johnson   Bernie   Parents

Antithesis: When a student starts to pester you, tell him. in any way that feels natural and comfortable, that he's O.K. as far as you are concerned, and that talking with him is O.K., but that you are on the job and can only allow 30 seconds a day per person for small talk. The "I'm busy, make an appointment" response is likely to be tainted with fed-up Parent feelings if the teacher has waited until he is pestered and annoyed. He should turn off the game at the beginning, before he can fill many stamp books and cash them in on an irritated "Go away."

22. High and Proud[*][31]

Clay, a high school senior, arrived at school with shoulder-length hair. He always appeared to have last shaved three days before. He often used four-letter words in front of teachers and administrators. He wore a shirt that had on it a picture of the American flag being stepped on. He openly talked about smoking marijuana, and he wore his shirt unbuttoned. He is well-equipped to bait the school authorities.

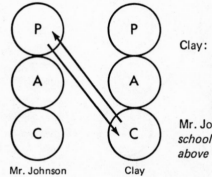

Mr. Johnson   Clay

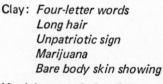

Clay: *Four-letter words*
Long hair
Unpatriotic sign
Marijuana
Bare body skin showing

Mr. Johnson: *Refers Clay to the school disciplinarian for the above five reasons.*

Mr. Johnson was forced either by his own Parent or the Parent rules of the school to react punitively, as in "Now I've Got You." The school code of conduct stated that there were to be no obscenities, no long hair on boys, no unpatriotic displays, no marijuana, and no open shirts. He took a loudly protesting Clay to the dean's office for punishment. Clay was provocative toward the dean and was expelled.

Objective evaluation does not show that long hair interferes with education. The same applies to shaving habits. Four-letter words offend those who wish to be offended. A picture of the flag being trampled on will not cause an inch of territory to be lost to an enemy. And as yet there is no scientific evidence that marijuana is more deleterious to health than cigarettes or leads to the use of harder drugs.

----

*Claude Steiner, the noted psychologist, first discovered and described this game.

Finally, everyone knows that the human body is a beautiful thing. Clay was able by these devices to cause grown-ups to over-react. This over-reaction made Clay a martyr and the administration the mean villain. The stronger the over-reaction the better for Clay. This type of reaction demonstrates that there is something wrong with the Parent-type person. "High and Proud" is the underdog's version of "Now I Got You." Instead of collecting enough evidence and having no one listen because he's the underdog, a "High and Proud" player will provoke an extreme situation in which the evidence against the enemy becomes unimpeachable. At this point a "reasonable public" will be aroused by the over-reaction and the "High and Proud" player wins.

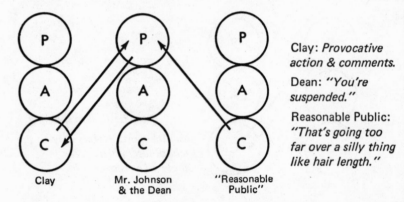

Clay: *Provocative action & comments.*

Dean: *"You're suspended."*

Reasonable Public: *"That's going too far over a silly thing like hair length."*

Clay   Mr. Johnson & the Dean   "Reasonable Public"

Antithesis: At the first provocation, don't over-react. Over-reaction is inevitably a Parent reaction. Also look at the situation being protested. If from the Adult point of view the prohibitions are unwarranted, either eliminate them or alter them. If the prohibitions, such as state laws, are out of your control, then explain the limits to the students, pointing out the obligations of the teachers and the administration.

23. Do Me Something[5]

Hermie's motto at school was "Here I am, Teacher, teach me." This was not an honest request but a challenge which Hermie intended to win by not learning anything. "You're the teacher. You're supposed to teach me something." The same steps can be repeated in "So I'm bad, change me."

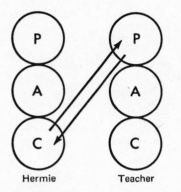

Hermie: *"Here I am. Teach me."*

Teacher: *"Here is the way I want you to do it."*

Hermie: *"I didn't learn nothing in your class."*

Teacher: *"Look How Hard I Tried."*

Antithesis: Mr. Johnson simply refused to use expressions such as "What *I* want you to do is," and "Do it *for me* by tomorrow."

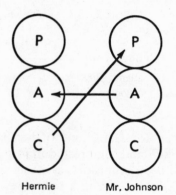

Hermie: *"I ain't learning nothing in your class."*

Mr. Johnson: *"What are you planning to do about that?"*

24. Stocking[5]

Diane walked in late to her class. She gave the teacher a late excuse from her counselor and sat down. She stood up looking down at her right side and in a voice audible to the people sitting around her she said, "Oh darn, my stocking has a run in it." The fellows around her got a free peek at her pulled-up skirt. The girls give her sour looks of the "There she goes again" type. She straightened her skirt and caught the fellows staring with silly grins on their faces. She turned away with a grimace that would wilt flowers on wallpaper.

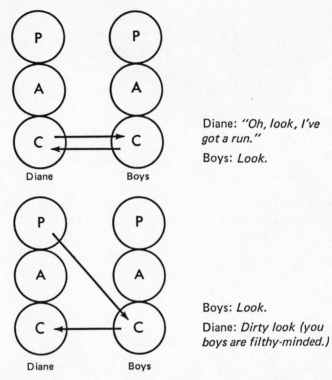

Diane: *"Oh, look, I've got a run."*
Boys: *Look.*

Boys: *Look.*
Diane: *Dirty look (you boys are filthy-minded.)*

These transactions reaffirmed for Diane one of her basic tenets of life: men are "all alike" and "interested in just one thing." She could just as well use a miniskirt, a sitting pose with legs apart, or a yawn and a stretch in a tight sweater. Any pose or posture that will encourage boys to stare will help her maintain her position that men are not O.K.

Antithesis: Mr. Johnson chose to have a woman teacher advise Diane that it's mostly up to a woman whether she is stared at in embarrassing positions. She took charge of six girls at the school and taught each such techniques as how to get in and out of sports cars while wearing short skirts.

25. Rapo[5]

Sheila Jo, playing a mild version of "Rapo," was in the hall at school and coyly lowered her eyes whenever Ray saw her looking at him. Ray caught the hint and worked his way over to her. Sheila Jo was watching his progress along with that of the other boys she was luring. As Ray came closer, Sheila Jo forgot about him, wondering why the others made little response. She strolled away to a place where she could be seen better and tried again. After ten minutes of trial and getting no more than a couple of casual glances, Sheila Jo became tired of this and left.

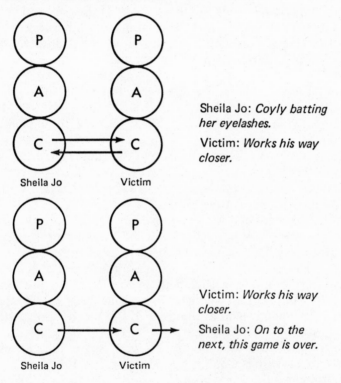

Sheila Jo: *Coyly batting her eyelashes.*

Victim: *Works his way closer.*

Victim: *Works his way closer.*

Sheila Jo: *On to the next, this game is over.*

Cheri, in a harder version of "Rapo," came in before class, sat down, and turned around to watch the boys come in the door. They talked about girls, baseball, and cars. She smiled sweetly at one of the boys and lowered her eyes demurely. He came over behind her, because she was sitting sideways. She brushed his hand as she moved around and turned to apologize and smiled at him. He pondered a moment, smiled a bit to himself, and leaned forward to whisper something to her. She gathered herself up in a huff and said "What do you think I am? Get lost!"

The difference between Sheila Jo and Cheri is that.Cheri makes more moves to get a different payoff. For Sheila Jo the payoff is watching the boy make his approach. For Cheri, the payoff is getting the boy into a position where she can tell him, "Get lost."

Sheila Jo's cousin, Bonnie Mae, played the hardest version of "Rapo." As a class hour ended everyone left except Bonnie Mae. She walked up to Mr. Johnson and sat provocatively on a desk in front of him. "Oh, Mr. Johnson, I was wondering if you could give me some of your time. I'm having some trouble with the math part of this business course."

"Well, I don't know, Bonnie Mae, I'm rather busy this week with correcting reports."

"I'd really appreciate a little of your time though, Mr. Johnson," she purred.

"How about the other teacher in the department, Miss Hoffenfeffer?"

"She can't explain like you do, Mr. Johnson. Couldn't you spare just a little bit of time? Please?"

Mr. Johnson looked around nervously as she moved a bit closer. She said, "Do you like gardenias? I just love the smell. Here, smell my flower." As he bent to smell the flower on her form-fitting sweater, he dropped the reports he was holding. Nervously he gathered them together off the floor. Gracefully and noiselessly she moved in beside him and helped him pick up the reports. A couple of times she brushed his arm.

"Please, Mr. Johnson, couldn't you spare just a few minutes this evening? Couldn't you, please, Mr. Johnson?"

"Well, I guess for a few minutes."

"Oh, thank you, Mr. Johnson. You don't know how much I appreciate this." She picked a piece of lint off his jacket. "Thanks again, Mr. Johnson."

During the next few weeks Bonnie Mae spent more and more time with Mr. Johnson. The extra help was given on an increasingly familiar level. She offered to stay after school and help with correcting papers. She arranged to stay after school to make up a test. She learned his schedule and walked past his room "by accident" when he was coming out of class. He gave her a ride home after class. She got a job babysitting for him. During the summer she cleaned house for him. They spoke on a first-name basis.

Bonnie Mae would now be able to tell her friends of some real or imagined incident involving physical contact. Her story could reach an alarmed mother, who could report what she had heard to the school authorities. A scandal or the teacher's forced retirement would follow.

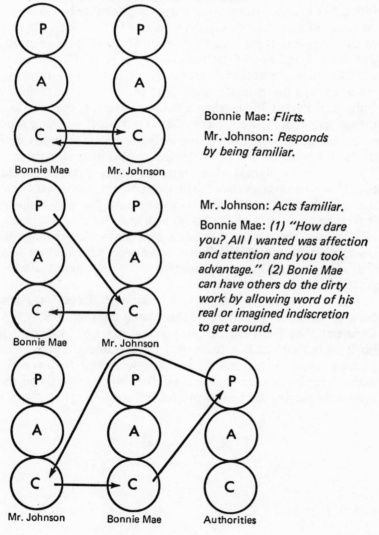

Bonnie Mae: *Flirts.*

Mr. Johnson: *Responds by being familiar.*

Mr. Johnson: *Acts familiar.*

Bonnie Mae: *(1) "How dare you? All I wanted was affection and attention and you took advantage." (2) Bonie Mae can have others do the dirty work by allowing word of his real or imagined indiscretion to get around.*

Antithesis: Maintain the Adult role of teacher and the occasional Parent role of support during working hours and with students. Avoid forms of familiarity which can be interpreted by a student as having sexual connotations. The teacher needs to keep his own sexy Child under strict control in cases such as those described.

Every person has territorial needs and there are four distinct zones of territory or living space.[21] There is , first, intimate distance, from touching to eighteen inches. There is personal distance, from eighteen inches to four feet. There is social distance, from four to seven feet. And there is public distance, from twelve to twenty-five feet. Each person is acutely aware, whether consciously or not, when someone intrudes into his intimate space, The teacher can sense on the Child and Parent levels when a student attempts to snare him into a game of "Rapo." The Parent gives off warning signs when someone not already on intimate terms intrudes, and the Child becomes irritated, uneasy, or excited. If a student does give sexy signals, one thing to do is to refer, in the course of the conversation with this student, to the fact that this is a classroom. Another way to remove the sexy element is to turn away part of the body. Still another way is to bring others into the group. Breaking eye contact or raising the voice to include others will also serve well. Still another way out of a potentially sexy situation is to talk about a wife, girlfriend, or fiancée.[16]

The student's antithesis to this version of "Rapo" has long been practiced in junior high schools and high schools. A boy finds out that a girl teases, tempts, and turns off. He will tell his friends that she is a tease, and if the same girl is referred to as a tease by several boys, they will tend to leave her alone. The boys who do seek out her company will be the ones who want to be teased and tossed aside.

IV

Teacher Games
Dealing with authority in yourself and others.

Identifying Teacher Games

Teacher games, like student games, can be categorized in several ways; here they will be divided into three varieties, with a chapter devoted to each:
1. "Close-to-Student" games, in which the Child ego state of the teacher wants strokes from the students.
2. "Helpful" games, in which the teacher's nurturing Parent ego state is predominant.
3. "I Know Best" games, played by the teacher's prejudiced Parent.

Learning the student's part in a game will take one only halfway to success. Few exciting sports have only one player or one team, and the teacher must learn to turn off games by not getting suckered into playing one of the parts himself.

Labeling a game and pointing it out to the other person is not turning off a game. It is only substituting the game of "Psychology"[5] and beating the opponent over the head with a new weapon.

Knowing how to properly label the hundred or more games is not important. What is important is understanding how to see the steps, how to reduce the frequency of the moves, and how to remove one or more of the steps of the destructive games in order to avoid a malicious payoff.

Most games are more likely to be generated when the teacher is in his Parent ego state, because the Child of a student can be triggered by the Parent of the teacher very easily. Some phrases that work especially well are:
> "You really should. . . ."
> "Why don't you. . . ."
> "The best thing is. . . ."
> "If only you would. . . ."
> "All right, children, let's all. . . ."

A classroom teacher has a contract for the year. His job description may include making lesson plans, providing supplemental material for the texts, planning research and study assignments, stimulating pupil-interest, giving personal guidance, and analyzing individual and group needs.[37] Anytime a teacher's personal feelings take precedence over, or are pursued at the expense of, these prescribed goals, then a game is in progress.

Education is most effective when the Adult does the programming. The Child should take an interest and lend enthusiasm, and the Parent should be approving. If the teacher's Parent does the talking, students can be pushed into rebel Child or compliant Child behavior. There are two Parent functions. One is nurturing, taking care of those in need; without this nurturing, no living human could have emerged from his initial helplessness. The other function is critical, or judgmental, and is learned from Parent tapes that have been available to us in our lives. These tapes are the clichés that the Parent part of us come up with automatically. They are sometimes of use, but they are nonadaptable and not related to the here-and-now. For example, if Mr. Johnson is irritated by Muriel's Child to the point where his Parent takes over, we will see what his own parents did under similar circumstances. If his own parents whined, then he probably will respond by whining. Under these situations much less education takes place.

Within his respective job description, a teacher must spend his time where he believes it will do the most good for the most students. This can mean an hour after school with one student and only two minutes with another. If a student or parent hollers "Unfair," he may be right in one sense. But true fairness does not require a teacher to divide his minutes on the job equally among his students. He may be doing his job the best possible way by a more thoughtful distribution of his time.

Mr. Johnson found that he was most successful when he made an individual contract with each student. "What do you want to learn or learn to do?" Such contracts need not cover all contingencies, and they can be renegotiated. But they do need to be firm or verifiable contracts.

CHAPTER 8

TEACHER GAMES: CLOSE-TO-STUDENT VARIETY

26. Buddy

Teachers who want to be liked by their students are playing
"Buddy" if their desire to be liked takes precedence over
classroom learning. A teacher who has within him a healthy,
fun-loving Child can use it to advantage in teaching.
Occasionally, however, a teacher who wasn't too popular in
his own school days tries too hard to be a pal. He will seem
phony in the eyes of the students, and some of his value as an
instructor will be lost.

Mr. Powell stopped Larry on campus often and talked to
him about personal things. Larry was popular at school; Mr.
Powell was a sideliner in his own school days, and he enjoyed
feeling like he was "in." He also talked with Sharon, the
best-liked and best-looking girl on campus. Sharon knew Mr.
Powell liked her and would let her hand work in late, help
her with her work, and give her the benefit of any doubt in
grading. Mr. Powell's Child felt that this would help his image
as a "Buddy," but his Adult knew that this was at the
expense of Sharon's academic interests. He was being paid
not to be "popular" but to teach.

Interest in students is potentially beneficial, and a student
generally does better in school, both academically and
in terms of behavior, when a teacher shows an interest in him
outside the classroom. The problem is that a teacher can be
more readily hooked into the potentially dangerous games,
like the trap-baiter games and sex games, outside the more
rigid structure of the classroom. If Mr. Powell knows his own
games, and knows the steps in the dangerous games, he can
be a buddy without playing "Buddy."

Antithesis: Have the Adult protect the Child. Let him have
fun but avoid danger. Mr. Powell lets his Child have fun,
explore, tease, and do all the things it wants; but at the same
time his Adult watches like a babysitter so that the Child
doesn't do anything that could lead to trouble. For example,
Mr. Powell might tell Bonnie Mae that she is very pretty. If

Bonnie Mae thanks him or teases him, then probably the transaction is fun and harmless. If Bonnie Mae starts moving in on his intimate space, Mr. Powell's Adult can protect him from a possible game of "Rapo," into which his Child might be drawn.

There are signals the student will offer if the teacher, or anyone else for that matter, comes too close and invades his space.[16] The preliminary signs are looking away, leg swinging, and tapping. These signs say "You're too close, too intimate." The next set of signals includes closing the eyes or looking down, tensing the shoulders, and pulling in the chin. If the teacher does not read the signals but continues the intrusion, the student will have to find some other way of getting away.

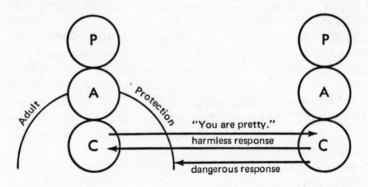

27. Self-Expression[5]

Mr. Freeman's English class discussed novels, and he encouraged each of his students to express himself on these novels. One story a student read was about a runaway. Mr. Freeman asked the boy about his life and urged him to tell how the story related to himself. Every indication of "Self-Expression" was encouraged as being healthy; "feelings are good."[5] Mr. Freeman listened with interest to everything that was said and his comments were "and what else?" "How did that make you feel?" "Tell me more."

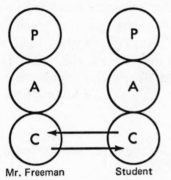

Student: *"I feel like . . . ."*
Mr. Freeman: *"Tell me more." (curious Child)*

On the other hand, Mr. Freeman might take a method his Child likes, such as "Self-Expression," and then try to justify it.

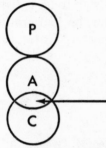

Overlapping area: *Mr. Freeman thinks his interest in details of students' lives is academically sound. The Child has control of that area and directs his actions for his own curiosity.*

A teacher saying, "Express yourself!" might be on educationally sound ground or it might be his curious Child prying. A check with the course objectives would tell which.

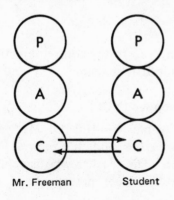

Mr. Freeman: *"How does that make you feel?"*
Student: *Gives intimate details.*

Antithesis: Educational objectives should be clear to both teacher and student from the start, so that each can determine the progress made. Anything within legal and social limits that furthers these objectives is O.K. Within the financial, social, and time limits Mr. Freeman finds the best ways to further these objectives. This is the Adult method.

28. Critique[5]

Teachers who play "Critique" see it as therapeutic. Students tend to see it as a waste of time.

Mr. de George thought of himself as a teacher to whom students could feel free to come for advice. His office was not usually filled, though. He encouraged certain students to tell him about themselves. He liked to listen to an individual describe his feelings and problems. Often he had groups of students expressing their feelings and giving "Critiques" of one another.

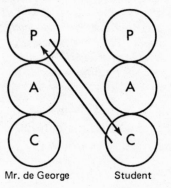

Mr. de George   Student

Mr. de George: *"What's the problem?"*

Student: *"Here it is."*

Mr. de George: *"Here's the judgment."*

Antithesis: In the classroom keep to the course objectives and avoid anything that does not further them.

29. You're Uncommonly Perceptive (YUP)[5]

YUP is the complementary game to "Lil Ol Me" and "Disciple." The teacher receives the student's interest and compliments as basically sincere. The teacher who is subject to the game thinks to himself, "How perceptive of the student to see what a good teacher I am." Most likely he is a good teacher, but he will be an even better one if he has an eye out for the "Disciple" who idolizes him, or the "Lil Ol Me" who wants to work him for a better grade.

Antithesis: See "Lil Ol Me," page 74.

CHAPTER 9

TEACHER GAMES: HELPFUL VARIETY

30. Student Folder

Miss Hulpfle noticed a boy who was quite aggressive in her classroom. He was often picking on other students.

"Aha, this boy needs my help!" smiled Miss Hulpfle. "If I can just figure out *the* reason why he's like this, I'll solve this problem. Perhaps it's his home life or an early trauma." She asked him several questions. "Do your parents argue much?" "Do you remember anything tragic in your childhood?"

Miss Hulpfle also went to the student's cumulative file folder in the front office. Here she went through the accumulated information on the boy and looked for *the* reason that he loved to argue and fight.

In most cases Miss Hulpfle finds nothing. This time she found a traumatic experience. She had "The Answer." She knew what "caused' the aggression. This was the end of her efforts. When the boy came up as a topic of conversation in the faculty room, Miss Hulpfle brought out the information as if it were an ancient treasure and said, "See, this is the reason."

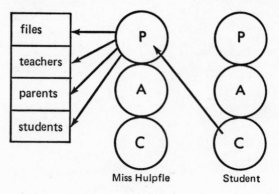

Student: *Hits someone, causing Miss Hulpfle to be concerned.*

Miss Hulpfle: *Goes through students cumulative folder to find "the" reason.*

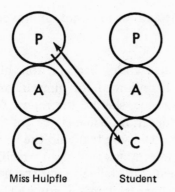

Miss Hulpfle   Student

Student: *Hits someone.*

Miss Hulpfle: *"I understand."*

Antithesis: Don't depend on finding "the" cause. Finding the game the student is playing is the key to finding an antithesis to his game.

31. I'm Only Trying To Help You (ITHY)[5]

Miss Marter, a school counselor, found out that Harry, a nice-looking, likable boy, was flunking several of his courses. She called him into her office, talked to him, and offered help.

"Would you like me to help you?"

"Sure," he answered quietly.

"I've talked to your teachers and have some extra assignments you can do to bring up your grades. Are you interested?"

"Yes."

"You'll need to go to the library and check out these five books."

"Okay."

"Check back in two weeks and let me know how you're coming along."

"Yeah."

Exit Harry. Three weeks passed. Miss Marter called in Harry again and asked, "How's the reading going?"

"They only had one of them at the library."

"Have you finished it yet?"

"I've read the first chapter."

"Well, go ahead and finish it and let me know in a week how you are doing."

"Okay."

A week later Miss Marter called Harry back in, told him the rest of the story that he hadn't read for himself, and helped him do the report. In essence, she did the report for him. He copied it over and handed it in. When Harry got the paper back it had a note saying, "Did you really do the work on this?" Harry showed it to Miss Marter. "I didn't realize that this would happen," she said. "I'll talk to your teacher. After this talk he handed the report back in and got a B+ on it. "Now he's on the right track," Miss Marter thought to herself. Two weeks later she asked his teachers how he was doing.

"Same as always. Nothing."

She stopped Harry in the hall the next day to ask what happened.

"Well, when my mom saw my paper she started after me, 'Why can't you do this all the time? I always told you if you'd buckle down and work hard you could get good grades. Well, young man, you don't have any excuse now, because I know you can do the work."

"What does all this make you feel like doing?" asked Miss Marter.

"Like flunking and getting back at her."

"What will you do?"

"I'm going to flunk my science test today anyway, so I'll take the paper home and hit her with that."

The following school day was Monday and Miss Marter asked what had happened.

"She yelled at me for a couple of minutes for flunking the science test but never mentioned staying home to study. So I guess I'm off the hook."

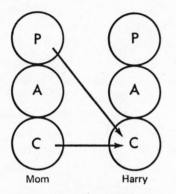

Mom: *Parent (social level)*
"Study and get good grades."

Mom: *Child (psychological level) "Fail."*

Harry went on, "Why knock myself out if I get hollered at more when I do the work than when I don't?"

"Oh, dear, I'm so sorry you've been yelled at so much. I Was Only Trying To Help You."

"You're a counselor and you're supposed to know these sort of things."

As he walked out Miss Marter feels a sense of frustration. This game is a complement of "Indigence."

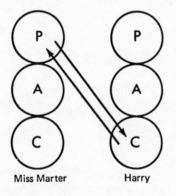

Miss Marter: *"Here, let me help."*

Harry: *"O.K."*

Miss Marter: *Helps.*

Harry: *"Your help didn't work."*

Miss Marter: *"I'm Only Trying To Help You." She is confused and frustrated.*

When Harry failed, his mother gave him strokes. A visit to Harry's home showed within a few minutes where the message was coming from. Harry's script included getting into trouble and failing in school.

Miss Marter and Harry's mother exchanged a few social amenities. Miss Marter said, "I would like to talk to you about Harry's schoolwork." Harry's mother laughed and said, "Well, tell me the worst. What has the rotten mess-up done now?"

This laugh is a gallow's transaction. A son's failure is not an appropriate time for a mother's laughter. If a relative or someone important to Harry laughs or smiles when Harry gets into trouble or fails, the message to him at the psychological level is reinforcement to continue the game.

Teachers who are always in their nurturing Parent also tend to keep the students unnecessarily dependent.[24]

Antithesis: The student can easily get out of this game by being independent and solving his own problems. If this Martyr "tries" to help Harry when he doesn't want or need help, Harry can listen and thank her for her efforts. Don't allow her to hook you into failing by her tempting and tantalizing guilt. So often it's difficult to resist disappointing somebody who carries around a sign, "Please don't disappoint me."

32. Sunny Side Up[5]

"Good morning," Miss Bright said to her second-grade class. "Isn't it a lovely day?" she beamed.

"But it's raining," said a boy in the front row.

"Isn't that wonderful? Rain makes the little flowers grow so we all have color to look at."

"Flowers give me hay fever," said a red-haired, freckle-faced, plump girl.

"Did you know that there's evidence of a relation between hay fever and intelligence? Maybe this means you're smarter than you thought you were."

She beamed and smiled through the day with the boys and girls, with her colleagues, and with her family at home. That evening she gulped down a couple of aspirin before going to bed.

These "Sunny Siders" aren't to be confused with optimists. An optimist feels good about life. A "Sunny Sider" tries to spread joy like a thick syrup over any words or actions that could possibly cause upset.

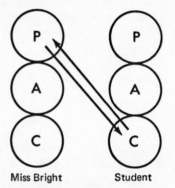

Miss Bright   Student

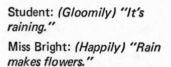

Student: *(Gloomily) "It's raining."*

Miss Bright: *(Happily) "Rain makes flowers."*

Antithesis: Stick to the contract of teaching. Don't waste time being a peacemaker or a happiness-spreader. Peacemakers keep arguments going[14] and happiness-spreaders drown spontaneity and inquisitiveness.

33. Education

Mr. Ed U. Kashen was disturbed when the third week of his fourth-grade class ground by. His students were climbing the walls. He took down his education mental hygiene books and looked through them for some answers. He knew that all would be better if he applied the principles of "Education" he had learned in college.

In the game of "Student Folder" the teacher looks for a cause for a student's actions. In the "Education" game the teacher looks for causes in the "atmosphere of the classroom."

Mr. Kashen changed the atmosphere of the classroom by opening with "quiet time." This helped for a while. Then the class was back to the old level. Next, bright bulletin boards. Again, temporary success. Later he tried letting the class out five minutes early but that was only successful for a while; other teachers complained because of the noise in the hall.

All children are experts at controlling their own parents, and all students bring this talent to school to use on their teachers. For a good example of the many techniques in raw form, sit in a class conducted by a timid substitute teacher.

Antithesis: "Get-On-With"[14] the business of teaching. If an incident occurs, figure out the game which means your own part and the student's part in it.

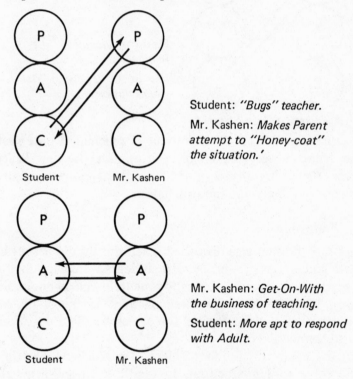

Student: *"Bugs" teacher.*

Mr. Kashen: *Makes Parent attempt to "Honey-coat" the situation.'*

Mr. Kashen: *Get-On-With the business of teaching.*

Student: *More apt to respond with Adult.*

34. Why Don't You — Yes But (WD—YB)[5]

"Why Don't You — Yes But" is really two complimentary games. The "Yes But" part has been examined in the section on student games. The "Why Don't You" teachers give suggestions and end up frustrated when these suggestions are not accepted or the suggestions are accepted and fail. This game is a form of "I'm Only Trying to Help You."

35. Look How Hard I've Tried[5]

Mr. Try was not certain that he was a good teacher. He was especially anxious to look good to the administration, the students, the parents, and the other teachers. If a student in his class didn't work, cut class, or made noise, he saw this as a put-down of himself. He tried hard to make such students behave and he tried hard to make them work. Each time he ended up failing and feeling frustrated.

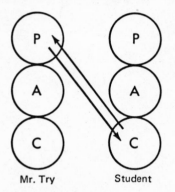

Mr. Try   Student

Student: *Doesn't work.*

Mr. Try: *Tried hard to help the student.*

The psychological level of these transactions is not so much the process of educating as it is "looking good" to others.

Antithesis: Keep firmly in mind what the objectives of the course are and what the job description of the teacher is. If a student insists on failing, he does so for a reason — to make someone angry, frustrated, or ill.

Many persons can play this game. Chuck's mother, for instance, goes by to see Mr. Try. She tells him how Chuck's grades are going down and lists all the measures she has taken to help Chuck to improve his grades. After all this effort, she exclaims to her husband, her friends, and now to the teacher, "Look How Hard I've Tried." This way she is off the hook and blameless.

If Chuck wants to switch from the game of "Indigence" to "Look How Hard I've Tried" (LHIT), he has several options. He can try hard but mess up. This can take the form of losing his work, or spending so much time on details that a minimum gets done.

If Mr. Try forces Chuck to write something as a punishment, he will balk (his rebel Child) and play "Stupid" or try hard and mess up with a "Look How Hard I've Tried."

There is little a teacher can do to solve home problems of this type. If the student plays the game, Mr. Try can let the student know in an Adult voice that he knows what is happening. This will at least turn off the game in that class. If the student finds that the teacher is playing the game, then he can decide not to be suckered into failing just to provide the payoff for the teacher's game.

CHAPTER 10

TEACHER GAMES: I-KNOW-BEST VARIETY

36. Furthermore[5]

Mr. Moore is upset with a student, and he cashes in the anger stamps he has been saving.

"You didn't bring a pencil and paper today."

"You forgot your book."

"You're always getting into trouble."

Each time the student answers, "I can explain," Mr. Moore pays no attention, but when the student pauses, Mr. Moore launches into his next accusation, which he may introduce with the word "Furthermore." This Parent-Child transaction is a common one in some schools.

The "Furthermore" player, a Parent-type, often intrudes into the student's territory or space. He leans over the student's desk, stands over him, perhaps shakes a scolding finger under his nose. By moving in and crowding him, or perhaps standing over him in a dominating position, the teacher challenges the student.[16] This challenge for superiority[11] from the teacher's Parent ego state may get immediate obedience, but sooner or later the student's angry rebel Child will get into the act. When a student is lectured at and accused, he will soon after begin to think of all the things he "should have said," and plan ways of getting even for the intrusion.

Antithesis: A student might as well stop trying to explain to a "Furthermore" teacher. He might better use the reflective listening technique, "I seem to be making you angry."

37. Tell Me This[5]

In some ways this is similar to the parlor game "Twenty Questions" or "You're Getting Warmer, You're Getting Colder." The psychology teacher Mr. Know, in discussing a case history, asked "What do you think will happen to this man if he doesn't change?" Each student offers a guess as to what might happen. Mr. Know already is certain that he has the answer and says "You're getting warmer," or "No, you're off base." Heuristic teaching can be very effective, but the integrity of the student must be respected if he is to grow intellectually. Talking to a student from the Parent ego state will encourage him to be a dependent Child. Better to respect the Adult of the student and watch it grow and develop.

38. Professional

A teacher who plays "Professional," Mr. D. Plomma, has a diploma to certify that he is a teacher, and he often tells himself, "Since I'm the teacher, if they don't learn, it's their own fault." This can bring many responses:

"Disciple": "Since you are the teacher, I'll learn from you."

"Uproar": "You're a lousy teacher and nobody likes you."

"Chip On The Shoulder": Any distracting statement will do.

"Stupid": "I don't understand."

"Make Me": "You can't teach me."

The way to make sure that this game doesn't get started is for the teacher to tell himself "I present what I've learned, using methods I've learned, in the hope that it will be of some use."

If Mr. Plomma has "a point he wants to get across," he is probably playing the game from his Parent ego state. These Parent points often contain phrases such as:

"Here is something interesting."

"Something that you have to realize is . . . ."

"Now this is important."

Parent points tend to be tedious or tricky. If he says, "I have these points to make today," he is more likely to trigger the disruptor games, which are effective at stopping the teacher from "getting the point across." Mr. Plomma's next move is to say, "You're just playing games." or "I don't want to play any of your silly games now." Here he would be using his critical Parent in a disparaging put-down.[14]

39. Why Did You — No, But (WD—NB)[5]

This is the other form of "Why Don't You — Yes But." In this case it is the teacher who wins and the student who goes off confused. In the "Why Don't You" game, a problem is presented, the teacher gives suggestions, the student refuses the suggestions, and the teacher is left frustrated. In "Why Did You — No, But" the teacher's position is that of a righteous Parent. This is a relative of "Now I've Got You."

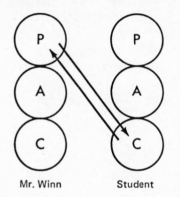

Mr. Winn

Student

Mr. Winn: *"Why didn't you turn in your work?"*

Student: *"Because you never told us."*

Mr. Winn: *"It's on the assignment board. Why didn't you look?"*

Student: *"Because I didn't have a chance."*

Mr. Winn: *"You didn't have one minute in the last six weeks to look on the board?"*

Student: *Silence, defeat, and confusion.*

Antithesis: The student's best protection is to be careful about due dates and rules of the class. Generally when a person's voice falls off to an almost inaudible tone it is because what he is saying isn't important; but in "Why Did You — No But" it can be a gimmick to catch a student off guard and draw him into the game. If a teacher suspects himself of playing this game he might insure against it by posting a plainly marked list of due dates and class rules. Also, he might have a student assistant remind the class at appropriate intervals before each assignment is due. Someone other than the teacher should select the student assistant.

40. Now I've Got You (NIGY)[5]

The teacher variety of "Now I've Got You" is common. All schools have a set of rules. Some of these come from the state, such as "no smoking" ordinances. Some come from the local school district, such as rules that students are not allowed to leave the school grounds during the school day. Some rules are individual school rules, such as a rule that no radios will be allowed on campus. Each of these rules, whether good or not, was enacted for a reason. A teacher plays "Now I've Got You" from the Parent position.

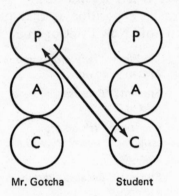

Mr. Gotcha: *"Don't let me catch you with a radio on campus."*

Student: *Brings a radio on campus.*

Mr. Gotcha: *"Now I've Got You."*

Mr. Gotcha   Student

Antithesis: If a teacher suspects himself of playing "Now I've Got You," he can begin to turn off the game by increasing the number of times he congratulates students for positive accomplishments and cutting down the number of times he seeks out infractions of rules.

Certain principals have been known to play this game, too. Mr. Prince I. Pal (from the game of "Blemish") sent out a note to all ninety teachers, stating that all incomplete grades are to be changed within two days or they will become F's. Halfway down the page of this notice is the statement, "If you have no changes to make, then turn in this paper with 'none' written across it." Mr Johnson read only the first paragraph, which stated "If you have any incompletes then they must . . . ." Since he didn't have any, and since he had to read twenty-five or thirty bulletins and memos a day, he •

threw the notice away. Two days later he received a copy of a letter, which was to be placed in his file, asking why he had failed to return the note, and requesting him to explain in writing why he was not able to do so.

Antithesis: First establish which persons in authority play "Now I've Got You," then be careful to have the Adult in charge of all dealings with these persons. Know the authority diagram of the school and the school district. Keep firmly in mind the job description and its legal limits as put forth in writing by the state, district, and individual school. One principal wrote the positive O.K. comments right on lesson plans and discussed in person the negative, not O.K. remarks.

41. See What You Made Me Do (SWYMD)[5]

Mr. Lohn is alone in his office correcting papers. He is deep in concentration, pondering one of them, when the door opens and a gust of wind blows the papers off his desk. He makes a grab for them and knocks a world globe onto the floor, breaking it. Joe, a student, walks in with a sheepish grin and says he's sorry. "See what you made me do?" thunders Mr. Lohn.

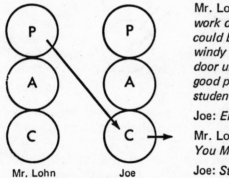

Mr. Lohn: *Arranged to work on something which could be disturbed on a windy day, leaving the door unlocked with the good posibility that a student would enter.*

Joe: *Enters.*

Mr. Lohn: *"See What You Made Me Do?"*

Joe: *Stays away.*

The payoff is that after a few SWYMD's students keep away from him.

Antithesis: For the student, learn to leave Mr. Lohn alone or make an appointment. For Mr. Lohn, begin to tone down the game by setting aside certain hours when he will be available by appointment or on a drop-in basis. Also, he can lock his door or retire to a private place when he doesn't want to be disturbed.

42. Courtroom[5]

"Mr. de George, he took my pencil and won't give it back," Jodi complains in class.

"That's a lie. It's my pencil. She borrowed it, and I need it," answers Jeff.

"Well, well," says Mr. de George, "Let's get to the bottom of this. What's going on here between you two?"

Mr. de George then hears evidence, accusations and perhaps testimony from other students, who might jump in as lawyers for Jodi or Jeff. The function of "Courtroom" is to allow Mr. de George to play God in the guise of a judge. He keeps "Uproar" games going.

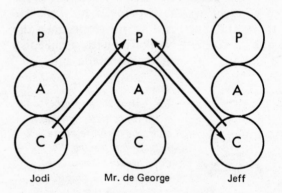

Jodi: *"He stole my pencil."*

Jeff: *"It's my pencil."*

Mr. de George: *"Let's hear both sides of this."*

Jodi   Mr. de George   Jeff

Peacemakers of this sort generally keep arguments going, whether in families, in counseling, in courtrooms, or in international politics.

Parents and teachers are often maneuvered into intervening, even by small children. One authority suggests the "bathroom technique,"[11] as an antithesis for this game: When two siblings begin arguing, the parent goes into the bathroom, locks the door, and waits until the argument is over. So far, no children have been lost in combat when this technique was applied.

In a school setting, nearly all arguments taken to the teacher can be solved satisfactorily without any interference from the teacher.

Mr. de George realized how he was being manipulated by the two students. The next time Jeff got angry and "accidentally" kicked Jodi, she screamed for help as usual. This time, however, Mr. de George merely said, "You seem to be upset." Jodi looked puzzled and asked, "Well, what are you going to do about it?" "Nothing," he said, "you're old enough to handle it by yourself."

Jeff wasted little time in testing this apparent permission to torture Jodi. Within the hour he got angry at her and hit her hard enough to give her a bloody nose. When there was no punishing reaction from the teacher, Jeff himself apologized by bringing Jodi a small present. In advanced cases, such as knifings, the only alternative is to send the students to the authorities.

If they are not careful the principal and the parents can be caught up in this game. One principal bragged about how "fair" he was because he would question the teacher at the same time he questioned the student "to get to the bottom of the problem" This procedure simply adds new players to the game.

43. Corner[5]

In this game the gimmick is responding literally to what is said rather than to what is clearly meant. Mr. X. Zack is working in his office. Beth, a bashful girl who has often turned work in late, walks in with a friend. She shyly asks Mr. Zack, "What do you think about papers being in on time?" Beth had finally got one in on time. Mr. Zack answered with a short Adult discourse on why it is more effective to have work in on time.

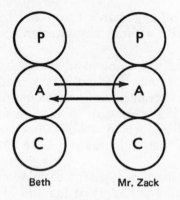

Beth: *"What do you think about prompt papers?"*

Mr. Zack: *"There are several advantages to promptness."*

Mr. Zack had responded to the explicit message, on the social level. But Beth's psychological or implicit message was "Give me a stroke for being a good girl."

Had he played the game he would have responded to her question, "What do you think about prompt papers?" by saying, "I think all papers should be in when due." This Parent reaction would ignore her need for strokes, and her response might be, "Gee, that's too bad; I never turn in papers on time, except this last one."

The teacher has now been had and is in the corner; she has played the game and he has lost his chance to stop it. His only reply will be a lame, "Well, uh, be sure you turn them in on time from now on." Because of his failure to provide positive strokes, she will not turn in papers on time in the future. She at least gets attention for her game playing.

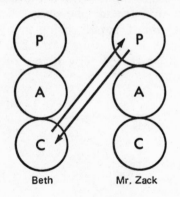

Beth: *"Tell me I've been a good girl for getting my work in on time."*

Mr. Zack: *"Good for you, I'm proud of you."*

Antithesis: The antithesis to this stroke-seeking and stroke-withholding game is to answer the implicit question. If Mr. Zack's wrinkled old grandmother comes to him and says, "How do I look today?" he wouldn't say "You look like a wrinkled old prune, Granny." Maybe she is as wrinkled as a prune, and maybe she did ask him to tell her how she looks, but Mr. Zack knows intuitively that this is not a question but a request for a stroke: "Tell me I look O.K.; tell me I *am* O.K." So he will say, "You look fine, Granny." If Mr. Zack can learn to trust his intuition he will heed his own Child's judgment and answer such implicit questions from students in the same way, with an appropriate stroke. Students looking for strokes quickly learn which teachers are adept at recognizing this, and they go to them for strokes.

44. It's Been Done Before[11]

In the guise of helping, Mr. B. Fore tells a student who has a bright idea that he should not get too excited. He says condescendingly that it has been thought of before and it is not a new idea.

Antithesis: If a student finds a teacher who regularly puts down bright ideas he should find another, more appreciative one.

CHAPTER 11

CONCLUSION

All games played in the classroom need not be turned off. The potentially dangerous or disruptive games, however, need to be minimized or eliminated when they are detrimental to educational objectives.

Most teacher — student games are Parent-Child trans-actions. With practice anyone can learn to spot the nurturing Parent voices, the punishing Parent voices, the free Child voices, the adapted Child voices, and the rebellious Child voices.

Another effective way to minimize game-playing in the classroom is to spell out what the contract is for each person involved. The contracts of the principal, vice-principal, dean, teacher, and other certified personnel are probably spelled out in some detail. But usually the contract for the student is simply to be physically present, what else is expected of him is left unclear. Mr. Johnson found that the method that worked best for him was to describe in writing the work needed for a certain grade. Anyone who wanted to negotiate beforehand the amount of work to be done was welcome. All students were notified of their progress biweekly. The number of "You never told us" complaints dropped to one or two a year. Having a contract helps focus attention on the work to be accomplished.

Knowing the name of a game is not important. The important thing is recognizing that something is going on besides the obvious transaction. Then you know there is an ulterior motive and thus a game. The Parent, Adult, and Child ego states are all O.K., and all necessary, and games are not in themselves bad and crooked. It is the payoff that determines what the game player is angling you to do. To avoid unpleasant games you can simply decline the opening move.

Appendix

APPENDIX

A BRIEF HISTORY OF TRANSACTIONAL ANALYSIS

Mel Boyce

Transactional Analysis was begun in 1954 by the late Eric Berne, M.D., a psychoanalyst. First in his writings and later with a small group of fellow scholars, Dr. Berne began to develop and explore a system of presenting complex ideas about human behavior in simple language. The basic approach was established in *A Layman's Guide to Psychiatry and Psychoanalysis* [3] (1957). Four more books followed in the next ten years. Classes were organized, lectures given, seminars formed, and Transactional Analysis (TA) bloomed, first in California and later throughout the United States and in other countries.

In 1964, Berne's *Games People Play* broke new ground and became an immediate best-seller. It has been published in fourteen languages to date and has sold over two million copies.

Since 1964, the system itself has been expanded and refined in seminars of professional workers. These men and women were originally students of Berne and later began to contribute ideas and to develop procedures dealing with a wide range of problems. The game concept soon found application in every walk of life. By 1966, TA seminars included alcoholism, drug addiction, obesity, organizational problems, race relations, juvenile delinquency, prison therapy, and education. Students came from across the United States, Canada, Latin America, India, England, Europe, and Africa. A paragraph from the Tenth Anniversary Bulletin of the Association gives this summary:

Millions of people in at least fifteen countries are now familiar with the principles of Transactional Analysis, due to the wide circulation and translation of its literature, and it is likely that 50,000 people have had personal instruction in it during the last ten years from our 500 or so active members. Formal clinical training is now entering its fourth generation, with students of the original students beginning to train other people. As recounted in the January 1963 issue of the Bulletin, the seed for all this was sown on February 18, 1958, when the first formal training session was held in San Francisco with six students attending, although informal discussions had been held for a few years before that at Mount Zion Hospital in San Francisco and in Carmel, California.

The TA concept of Parent, Adult, and Child ego states is based in part on Freud's postulation of a Superego, Ego, and Id. Freud refers to the Superego as the parental authority and the bearer of culture from previous generations. He says further, "I cannot tell you as much as I could wish about the change from the parental functions to the superego, partly because the process is so complicated, and partly because we do not feel we have fully understood it." Berne has developed the concept of a Parental ego state in great detail, dividing the Parent into the Prejudiced or Critical side and the Nurturing side, and he has shown in detail the way in which a child receives intact certain parental concepts from his elders. Ego states are made obvious by gestures, body postures, type of language, and words used. Parental statements usually contain qualifiers, such as "because" and "therefore." "Prejudiced" means one has accepted ideas without evaluating them, and such ideas include many handed down from ancestors.

Freud refers to the Ego in two ways: first, as a concept of total personality, and second, as a central part of that personality which contains "an observing function . . . and stands for reason and circumspection." Berne has clarified the Ego function, calling it the Adult, and has expanded the idea of freeing and strengthening it until the Adult generally has "executive" control of the personality. Adult statements are matter-of-fact, calm, and direct, such as "Yes," "No," and "I'm going downtown."

The remarkable Id of Freudian thinking is another sort of concept. Freud ascribes to it such qualities as "instinctual impulses" and such negative traits as "no values, no good and evil, no morality," but he says that the Ego "borrows its energy from the Id."

Berne has formalized the Id concept as the Child ego state, with an Adapted or perverse side and a Natural or happy side. When the adapted Child is trying to play a game, it is usually a "con" operation. The voice is strained, or too loud or too soft, the gestures are imploring, threatening, or random. The statement or question is usually "beside the point" and is calculated to arouse reaction rather than to communicate ideas clearly. The natural Child seeks pleasure, is creative, learns rapidly, and is spontaneous. Berne's structural diagrams are more precise than Freud's. But both men agree that much of the functioning of the mind is unconscious, so that we can necessarily diagram and describe accurately only the conscious part.

Games are only a part of the TA system. They relate to transactions (exchanges between people) that have ulterior, or hidden, motives. Technically, these usually occur between a Parent ego state and a Child ego state. Transactions can be of several kinds, ulterior or crossed, parallel or complementary. "A game," says Berne, "is an ongoing series of complementary ulterior transactions progressing to a well-defined predictable outcome."[5]

In 1960 the Transactional Analysis Association (later the International Transactional Analysis Association) was chartered under the State of California, and numerous chapters, usually called Institutes, have been organized. Observations made in a Calcutta mental hospital can now be related meaningfully to experiences in a U.S. Naval Hospital or an out-patient clinic in Tahiti.

At this juncture, it is important to note that Transactional Analysis does not differ with or depart from other established systems, except in emphasis. Thus, a scholarly approach is indicated, so that practioners can learn from each other and theorists can be free to follow whatever paths their researches point out. On the other hand, TA people insist that all concepts be thoroughly tested in practice and over a period of time. Many advocates of TA find themselves also embracing the procedures of non-directive, existential, gestalt, behaviorist, and here-and-now therapy. In short, TA-trained people tend to be eclectic, direct, and specific, but also pragmatic in their approach.

There are many references, although brief ones, to the concepts of TA in both popular and technical literature. Almost daily references to "games" occur in periodicals and books. While many of these refer in fact to what TA calls "pastimes" and "operations," they attest to the popularity and aptness of this method of viewing human nature. In fact, the whole system of games is based upon close observation of behavior. A person who puts down the daily newspaper to exclaim "Ain't it awful how people are acting today" is cogently naming a popular game, and all its future maneuvers, moves, and plays are implicit in his statement.

References/Bibliography

REFERENCES/BIBLIOGRAPHY

1. Ardrey, Robert. THE TERRITORIAL IMPERATIVE. Atheneum, New York, 1966.
2. Berne, Eric. HAPPY VALLEY. Grove Press, New York, 1968.
3. _____. A LAYMAN'S GUIDE TO PSYCHIATRY AND PSYCHOANALYSIS. Simon and Schuster, New York, 1957.
4. _____. TRANSACTIONAL ANALYSIS IN PSYCHO-THERAPY. Grove Press, New York, 1961.
5. _____. GAMES PEOPLE PLAY. Grove Press, New York, 1964.
6. _____. THE STRUCTURE AND DYNAMICS OF ORGANIZATION AND GROUPS. Grove Press, New York, 1965.
7. _____. GROUP TREATMENT. Grove Press, New York, 1970.
8. Birdwhistle, R. L. EXPRESSIONS OF THE EMOTIONS IN MAN. International Universities Press, New York, 1963.
9. Campos, Leonard, and Paul McCormick. INTRODUCE YOURSELF TO TRANSACTIONAL ANALYSIS. San Joaquin Transactional Analysis Study Group, Stockton, California, 1969.
10. Cats, Jacob; OFFICIUM PUELLARUM, IN CASTIS AMORIBUS: Emblemate Expressum; Tot Middleburgh, Ghedruckt by Hans Vander Hellum: 1618.
11. Dreikurs, Rudolf. CHILDREN THE CHALLENGE. Duell, Sloan and Pearce, New York, 1967.
12. Ernst, Franklin H., Jr. THE ACTIVITY OF LISTENING. Foundation for Group Treatment, P.O. Box 1141, Vallejo, California, 1968.
13. _____. LEAVING YOUR MARK. F.G.T.; P.O. Box 1141, Vallejo, California, 1968.
14. _____. Encounterer. F.G.T., Box 1141, Vallejo, California, 1969-70.

15. Ernst, Kenneth J. AMETHYSM. 4289 Alder Avenue, Fremont, California, 1953.
16. Fast, Julius. BODY LANGUAGE. M. Evans and Co., New York, 1970.
17. Fremont Unified School District; JOB DESCRIPTION FOR HIGH SCHOOL TEACHERS: Fremont, California, 1969.
18. Freud, Sigmund. NEW INTRODUCTORY LECTURES ON PSYCHOANALYSIS. W.W. Norton & Co., New York, 1933.
19. Glasser, William. REALITY THERAPY. Harper & Row, New York, 1965.
20. _____. SCHOOLS WITHOUT FAILURE. Harper & Row, New York, 1969.
21. Hall, Edward T. MAN'S IMAGE IN MEDICINE AND ANTHROPOLOGY. International Universities Press, New York, 1963.
22. Hamilton, Edith. MYTHOLOGY. Mentor Books, New York, 1953.
23. Hildebrand, Milton, and Robert Wilson. EFFECTIVE UNIVERSITY TEACHING AND ITS EVALUATION. Academic Senate, University of California, Davis, California, 1969.
24. James, Muriel, and Dorothy Johgeward. BORN TO WIN. Addison Wesley Publishing Co., Menlo Park, California, 1971.
25. Karpman, Steven. DRAMA TRIANGLE, SCRIPT DRAMA ANALYSIS. Transactional Analysis Bulletin. Vol. 7, No. 26. International Transactional Analysis Association, 3155 College Avenue, Berkeley, California, 1968.
26. Levine, S. STIMULATION IN INFANCY. Scientific American, 202: 80-86, May 1960.
27. Ortega y Gasset, Jose. MAN AND PEOPLE. W.W. Norton & Co., New York 1957.
28. Scheflin, A. E. "SIGNIFICANCE OF POSTURE IN COMMUNICATION," PSYCHIATRY, Vol. 27, No. 4, November 1964.

29 Schutz, William. JOY, Grove Press, New York, 1967.
30. Spitz, Rene. "HOSPITALISM: GENESIS OF PSYCHI-ATRIC CONDITIONS IN EARLY CHILDHOOD," Psychoanalytic Study of the Child. 1:53-74, 1945.
31. Steiner, Claude. GAMES ALCOHOLIC PLAY, Grove Press, New York, 1971.
32. _____. "STROKE ECONOMY" Transactional Analysis Journal, Vol. 1, No. 3. July 1971.
33. _____. "FUZZY TALE." Transactional Analysis Bulletin, Vol. 9, No. 30, Oct. 1970.
34. _____. "STROKE ECONOMY," Transactional Analysis Journal, Vol. 1, No. 2, 1971.
35. Transactional Analysis Bulletin. Vol. 7, No. 25, January 1968, Carmel, California.
36. Transactional Analysis Bulletin. Vol. 6, No. 21, January 1967.
37 United States Government. Department of the Army, Form DA 374.

OTHER BOOKS FROM CELESTIAL ARTS

PRE-SCRIPTION
A TA Look at Child Development
Ken Ernst
158-2 $4.50

FEELINGS: Inside You and Outloud Too
Barbara Kay Pollard
06-3 $4.95

JAPAN: Customs and Culture
Duane Rubin
04-7 $4.95

EVERYWOMAN'S GUIDE TO COLLEGE
Eileen Gray
903-6 $3.95

ALPHA BRAIN WAVES
David Boxerman and Aron Spilken
16-0 $4.95

WILDFLOWERS OF THE WEST
Mabel Crittenden and Dorothy Telfer
069-1 $4.95